THE NAUGHTY NINETIES

THE
NAUGHTY
NINETIES

FOOTBALL'S COMING HOME?

MARTIN KING AND MARTIN KNIGHT

MAINSTREAM
PUBLISHING

EDINBURGH AND LONDON

Reprinted, 2007

First published in Great Britain in 1999 by
MAINSTREAM PUBLISHING COMPANY (EDINBURGH) LTD
7 Albany Street
Edinburgh EH1 3UG

ISBN 9781840181913

A catalogue record for this book is available from the British Library

Typeset in Garamond
Printed and bound in Great Britain by
Cox & Wyman Ltd, Reading

Contents

This book is dedicated to my mum, Rene King, who died suddenly on 5 January 1999. A real character sadly missed by all her family and friends.

God bless, Mum – Martin and Alan

Goodbye good friend
God rest good friend
God bless good friend
God loves.

Acknowledgements

Martin King and Martin Knight would like to thank Irvine Welsh for the introduction and for telling it how it really is. Thanks too to John King for his continued enthusiasm, support and advice. Cheers, John. The authors would also like to apologise to the many people who said they would have liked to have featured in *Hoolifan* but didn't, and to the few people who did feature but would rather not have.

Martin King would like to thank Mandy, Kortney and Rory-Ben for their encouragement, brother Alan, his family and the rest of the King clan. Thanks also to Dr Gary Armstrong, Kenny Goodwin, Tony Roffey, Linda and David for being so supportive, Jason and Marcus, Chrissy Porter, Terminator John, Peb and Brian, Swansea Paul and Joe, Michael, Debbie, Jackie, Karen, Helen, Dave Nunn, Magic Johnson, Martin, Mickey Price, the three Andys, Bruno, Mario and Glen, Carl, West Ham Glen, Mark McBride, Alfie, Nigel, Jimmy – Sutton United's star player, Sugar Puff, Bob, Pear Brewley, Nick, Steve Hawkins, Mekon Paul, Malcolm, Gary Chivers, Nick, Carol and Dave, Nigel and Ian, Jerry Kilburn, Black Jimmy, LeRoy, Winston and Delroy, Dawn, Rob, Jo-Anne, Kevin, Anne and Brian, Graham the chef, Carl, Lisa, Mark, Debbie, Hattie and Ted, Alfie and Jack-Jo and Dave Councillor, Kev Welling and Sue, his first lady of Bognor, Kim, Mark, Laura, Stacey, Billy, Danielle, Neil, Wendy, Harry, Eileen, Jerry, Ben, Chris and Jerry, Alex and

James, Tony C and Colin Daniels, the Lyons and the King mobs, Janice, Joyce, Sue, Siddy and Gladys, Fat Pat, Paul from Reading, Giles and the Manning twins. Finally, thanks to everyone who bought *Hoolifan* and to all of those people who could have grassed me up to the Child Support Agency but didn't.

Martin Knight would like to thank Val and the kids.

Introduction by Irvine Welsh

You can almost hear the loud, repetitive bleats from the book reviewers already: 'Oh, God, not another football hooligan (or drugs or music or rave) book. Hasn't that been done by one of our chaps already? Yes, this was all well and good for a while, but now it's getting rather out of hand.' Much of this attitude stems from the traditional fear the Establishment in Britain has of contemporary working-class violence, especially when it's collectively expressed. Thus the same newspaper pundits who get all stiff and moist over biographies of bare-knuckle fighters often turn a bit squeamish at the thought of two mobs having it in public streets with not a purse in sight for the victor.

Another inference, of course, is that it's time to leave the writing to 'real' writers, whether they be academics or people who went to public school or Oxbridge and who hang around the appropriate salons, like the Groucho or Soho House. The problem, of course, in doing that is that you're leaving it to people who know absolutely nothing about it.

The most important thing for me about writing is that people should be able to express a view on their own culture from inside that culture, and by doing so take responsibility for it. Taking responsibility doesn't mean answering to some media whore with an inflated sense of their own importance, but instead answering to your own peers. That's exactly what Martin King and Martin Knight have done, first with *Hoolifan* and now with *The Naughty Nineties*.

The first book became, in John King's words, an instant 'terrace-culture classic'. Not only did the authors prove that they could talk the talk as well as walk the walk, they also showed that they could talk it with more intelligence, insight and humour than just about anybody else who's put pen to paper on the subject. *Hoolifan* argued convincingly about the institutionalisation of 'football hooligan culture', whereby all parties – police, media, academics, even the hooligans themselves – have had a vested interest in sensationalising what's going on. What was most heartening about the book was the signal that so many ex-crew members are putting egos aside and realising that a rigorous pursuit of the truth boosts rather than diminishes reputations. In *Hoolifan*, many of the police- and media-generated myths surrounding the use of weapons, racism, Nazism and clandestine organisations were squarely dealt with and those perpetuating that kind of nonsense from a position of ignorance were taken to task.

By taking responsibility for rewriting football culture, the authors have resurrected the names of many working-class heroes, names which would otherwise have been lost to future generations. This shouldn't happen. History is history. It's for all of us, from every class and every culture, and is thus far too important to be left to those with a purely élitist take on the world.

As a phenomenon, football hooliganism has been tremendously durable and far too widespread to have been merely the antics of a so-called 'mindless minority'. In fact, it strikes me that just about every male I know, and quite a few females, between the ages of 16 and 60 have had their lives touched by it in one form or another. From organising top-level violence to running with a mob, throwing the odd punch, mouthing off, running from a mob, observing calmly or in terror from the sidelines, sitting in the pub issuing knee-jerk cries of condemnation or alternatively basking in the quiet satisfaction that 'our boys' acquitted themselves well, we've all been involved at some time, at some level. And often at different levels over different times. The truth is that from 'generals' to bit-part players to extras, spectator aggro at football has been an integral part of working-class youth and adult life for decades.

I was reading recently about a major football riot involving two partisan mobs. Although there was sustained violence before, during and after the match in question, only four arrests were made on the day. This wasn't enough for the local and national media, who demanded that something be done about it. In response, and following 'intelligence' received – i.e. information from grasses – the local police mounted a series of dawn raids resulting in numerous alleged perpetrators being arrested and subsequently receiving stiff custodial sentences. This wasn't the ill-fated Operation Own Goal; it was Greenock Morton v. Port Glasgow Athletic at Cappilow one hundred years earlier.

I went fairly regularly to Chelsea over a few seasons in the late '70s and early '80s. When I first moved to London I lived in west London and tended to alternate between the different atmospheres of Stamford Bridge and Loftus Road. My first visit to the Shed was in 1978 with a pal from Glasgow, who supported Rangers, and several other friends, dyed-in-the-wool Chelsea who lived at various stop-off points along the Uxbridge Road. I'd been looking forward to seeing Chelsea since watching the 1970 Cup final win over Leeds. Of course, things had moved on a bit, and not for the better. The boyhood TV visions of Osgood and Cooke had been replaced by the more prosaic talents of Langley and Aylott as Chelsea wallowed in what the authors describe in *Hoolifan* as 'the shit years'.

But the excitement in attending any game at any ground in Britain in your youth in those times was generated by the whole package: mates, pub, banter, match and, let's be honest here, the real or imagined prospect of a little bit of anarchy. Although I had, and still have, no partisan loyalty to any of the London clubs, I've particularly enjoyed the atmosphere at West Ham, Millwall and Chelsea more than at any of the other grounds. They may have been the most troublesome as far as hooliganism went, but I remember much more vividly the raucous support and the banter as being similar to what I'd been used to at Scottish games. The other London grounds never really did it for me.

All clubs and their supporters have certain unique features and Chelsea are no exception. Their following, though strongest in west and south-west London, tends to be more dispersed throughout the south-east of England than that of the other main London clubs. Arsenal and Spurs fans are indelibly associated with north London and its suburbs and dormitory towns, whereas West Ham are unmistakably out of east London and its Essex diaspora and Millwall are concentrated in the south-east of the city. (It may seem strange to some people that I regard Millwall as a 'major' London club. The fact is that, in terms of football culture, they are a major *British* club.) Against all this, for many die-hard Chelsea fans (which now usually means the ones who either can't afford a season ticket or don't like the cricket-style atmosphere) spread in pockets across the shires, Chelsea *are* the community.

That community-of-club-in-itself rather than club-as-representing-the-area vibe is probably one of the reasons why some of the same faces crop up throughout the decades at Chelsea, giving a sense of continuity. From the end-taking '70s, through the outside-the-ground battles of the '80s, to the more organised and underground meets of the '90s, there are probably more people who've done the lot on a regular basis at Chelsea than at any other club in Britain. At most clubs (Hibs, for example), a mob will get together at some point, then fade away. Thus the '80s casuals might have little knowledge of or contact with the often district-gang-based scarfer mobs of the '70s and late '60s.

In many of the dormitory towns in the south-east, there is no real clubland structure or music scene to melt into, so for those who like the crowd, the social focus is on the club supported. This is probably why, as the authors wrote in *Hoolifan*, Chelsea always obliged, they always turned out. I recall a Hibs–Chelsea friendly where the disappointment of the Hibs crew that two buses of Chelsea boys had been stopped at the border and sent back was evident. The interesting thing was that some of the Hibs boys were not only disappointed for themselves, but also for the Chelsea fans. One well-known Hibs face told me, 'I felt sorry for the Chelsea boys. I've heard they always like to put on a show, so they'll be gutted to be turned back after coming all that way.'

Many people will find the solidarity that exists between crews who want to do each other damage quite strange. While the potential for silly personal vendettas to get out of hand always exists (and perhaps more so in the '90s), it's generally the case that people who have shared similar experiences tend to get on, and football punters are no different in that respect.

When the '90s kicked in, a conventional wisdom grew that football violence had all but vanished, or was at least seriously marginalised. The Taylor Report and the attendant increased security and all-seated stadia had taken their toll. The North Bank, the Shelf and the Shed had been 'taken' for good, not by rival mobs but by redevelopment and thirty-something yuppies with their credit cards and their pristine copies of *Fever Pitch*. In some underground writing, a lot was made of the effects of acid house and the Ecstasy revolution and how many top terrace faces got to know each other as friends on the dancefloors of the nation's clubs. While that undoubtedly did happen, in some ways it probably helped pave the way for the more designer violence of the '90s.

Because people were in contact with each other socially through clubland, they were able to organise meets further from the ground. It was possible for groups to party together one Saturday night, then fight viciously the next. The unpalatable truth for many commentators who habitually demonise football hooligans as a matter of course is that most of the consenting young (and sometimes not so young) adults who choose to meet up and kick fuck out of each other are among the most decent and moral people around, and many (though not all) of them would never dream of being violent in any other social context.

The idea of 'safety' following Hillsborough has been the Trojan horse for the clubs who have systematically ripped off their working-class support for years, rebranding 'soccer'. The line frequently trumpeted by the authorities is that 'lessons have been learned after Hillsborough'. What offensive, disgusting nonsense this is, especially given how the supporters involved were treated then and have been treated since by the Establishment. Hillsborough was no different from other football disasters involving poor facilities, bad policing and loss of life except that it took place in the television age. The lessons were learned, all right, but they were lessons in political opportunism and commercial exploitation and they were learned by a nouveau-ponce class who took the opportunity to seize control of the game at the top level.

It is now obligatory for any politician or media personality worth his salt to declare a 'passionate support' for some club or other. During Euro 96 and France 98 especially, the Prime Minister of Cool Britannia was fond of declaring his 'passionate support' for Newcastle United. Did this 'passionate support' develop when he was an Edinburgh schoolboy, an Oxford student, a Hackney councillor, or when he got selected for a safe seat in the north-east of England? I only ask. The fact is that the yuppification of the game has progressed to such an extent that football is now seen as a game only for the middle classes and more affluent working-class people in family groups to attend. Younger working-class kids, or men who like to attend games in a group with their friends, are expected to couch potato the experience through satellite-television subscriptions or nip to the pub and boost their local landlord's coffers. People will accuse me of hypocrisy here, as I can afford the best seats, as can many who grumble in this way. This misses the point about football being a social event, that point being that I want to go to matches with the people I've always gone to them with. I don't really want to spend Saturday afternoon (or whenever TV allows it) sitting next to some cricket fan who's going undercover in a replica shirt.

One thing I've noticed throughout the '90s has been a change of attitude in the so-called 'ordinary fan'. This is the mysterious creature often evoked but seldom analysed, whom we were constantly told was 'sick of the violence in football'. This was undoubtedly true, but as this book and *Hoolifan* both point out, as football hooliganism evolved and the rules of engagement between the participants became more defined, the chances of the 'ordinary fan' being caught up in such incidents decreased exponentially. Nowadays, if the 'ordinary fan' is sick of anything in football, it's the fact that he or she can no longer afford to see their favourite club on a regular basis.

It's not so strange that this particular 'sickness', which is expounded regularly in every pub the length and breadth of the country, is seldom trumpeted in the media. Not when you consider the influence they have in the game. If they do deign to mention this discontent, it's generally to patronise or dismiss as dinosaurs people who have the temerity to say they've been priced out of the game. But they have been, and they're all ages and races and both sexes. Even when Manchester United's stadium's capacity is increased to sixty-seven thousand, you can rest assured that young kids from Blakeley, Ardwick Green or Salford still won't be able to go along and watch their club like they could not so many years ago. And you won't see many schoolkids from Acton or Hayes filling the seats at Stamford Bridge.

In the '90s, the media now finally seem as aware as the supporters and, to be fair, the sociologists who've been saying for about twenty years that the levels and content of reporting can influence levels of fan aggro. Post-Hillsborough, where the horrific deaths of Liverpool fans were shamefully blamed by the authorities and sections of the media on the supporters themselves, rather than on the inept and subsequently corrupt policing, part of the systematic attempt to rebrand football has involved talking down the level of perceived crowd violence. As the book suggests, as a strategy for quelling the swedging, this has been as effective as reporting it luridly was for pumping it up in the '70s and '80s. Now a serious row could be taking place in a ground and from your television screen you'd never know it. You'd be looking at images of face-painted kids (aah!) or pretty young women (phwoar – sexy football!).

While West Ham, Chelsea and Millwall drew a lot of their strength from the relative difficulty in policing London as opposed to other cities due to its sheer size, they were undoubtedly given a recruitment fillip by the over-reporting of the London-based British media. In Scotland in the '80s, the Hibs and Aberdeen crews earned a great deal of notorious credibility in the same way, as the Glasgow-based media in the late '80s were hyping up a sanitised Glasgow (at the expense of the east-of-Scotland cities) in preparation for its status as European City of Culture 1990. We were asked to believe that those east-coast thugs in designer gear who all attended Fettes with Tony Blair and enjoyed royal garden parties at Balmoral were running riot, while Celtic and Rangers fans had metamorphosed into advertising executives or golfing suburbanites from Newton Mearns who'd never sung a note of a sectarian song in their lives.

As *Hoolifan* and now *The Naughty Nineties* illustrate, football fans revelled in this notoriety, often using the media to get their exploits across. Many people involved in football violence have delighted in playing the pantomime villains to wind up the media. A theatrical Nazi salute à la John Cleese for the cameras here, a bit of Dot Cotton- or Vera Duckworth-style contrived, salacious gossip about clandestine cells and ruthless generals there; it all makes good copy and feeds the myth. It has long been a source of amusement for those who were there to sit back and relax with the Sunday papers and see just how wrong the press got it. The implication of one hilarious chapter in this book is that the University of Leicester should seriously consider presenting some fans in their locale with honorary degrees in media studies. It's maybe a coincidence, but a lot of the sillier academic studies on hooliganism came out of Leicester University. Perhaps some other university's research department might want to commission a study into what makes people living in Leicester particularly predisposed to believing nonsensical myths about football mobs.

Such myths fed into the media by wind-up merchants often seemed to come back like boomerangs into football culture. Many gang names like Headhunters, Bushwhackers, Capital City Service, Blades Business Crew and so on probably didn't exist until somebody invented them in the pub for the benefit of a journalist, and in all likelihood they only became common currency after being reappointed (usually with heavy irony) by the crews as a result of the ensuing article.

However, media embargoes on the reporting of football violence may not be that effective in the long run, as relevant word-of-mouth, always the best and most trustworthy medium, implacably suggests an upswing in activity. As the two Martins' book points out, the violence has not gone away, it's just become more specialised and involves a more dedicated hard-core of participants. Yet, in tandem with this, there would seem to be the potential for a return to large-scale football violence in Britain with more long-standing fans, including those who may have had little involvement in hooliganism, now more disaffected and alienated from the senior game than ever. This would seem particularly the case at mediafest international tournaments. The authorities, the clubs and the media companies have, I feel, underestimated the passion of people for whom the game is, and always will be, a social rather than a consumer or a 'leisure' package. Maybe it's because I'm writing this after attending a West Ham–Leeds game where I witnessed not mobs but replica strips having a set-to, having watching the Celtic–Rangers game on television the following day, with some stories of a recent Millwall visit to Man City still ringing in my ears, but I get the distinct impression that football violence may be, as the authors tentatively suggest, coming home again.

The Naughty Nineties takes up where *Hoolifan* left off, examining some major confrontations from the perspectives of the main players and contrasting them with the broader societal reaction which is largely determined by the media and the authorities. As with its predecessor, this book is written with great wit, insight and that often self-deprecating humour which beautifully captures the real terracing camaraderie and inimitable style of the British working classes at deadly serious play. And for writers from a section of the community which is often ridiculously portrayed as having a sinister, clandestine agenda involving something akin to the setting up of thousand-year Reichs, the conclusions of *The Naughty Nineties* are inevitably libertarian, based on common sense, experience and notions of natural justice. And those are qualities which are not exactly evident in abundance in those who control the game in Britain today.

As in the case of, say, drugs, or perhaps mountaineering, in a free society some people will always choose to partake in activities which involve both excitement and risk. The appeal of illicit pleasure always runs high. As my grandmother would have said, 'as long as they're not bothering anybody else'. And if they are, I get the sneaking feeling that the 'anybody elses' being bothered are increasingly not the so-called 'ordinary fans' but those who have made, and are still making, an absolute killing out of football. And, as they say, whose game is it anyway?

IRVINE WELSH

The Dream

'The car's here! The car's here!'

Mandy is not doing a very good job of containing her excitement. She shouts this to me up the stairs in between fussing around the baby-sitter, telling her about the Coke and crisps that are in the kitchen and that we've got our mobile with us in case she needs to call.

'All right, I'm coming. I'm just trying to put on this poxy dickey bow,' I say, walking down the stairs struggling with my bow tie. 'Why you bought me a velvet one I'll never know.'

'Because they look smart and that's what you're meant to wear with your dinner suit. That's what the man in the hire shop said, anyway.'

'Well I feel like Frank fucking Muir with this thing round my neck.'

Mandy pushes me gently in front of the mirror hanging in the hall.

'See. Look how nice you look.'

Unconvinced, I usher Mandy out of the door and down the lift to the stretch limousine that is waiting for us. The driver is kitted out in a grey suit, black cap and leather gloves and he's holding the door open for us. I don't feel such a prick now.

'Do your flies up,' I say, nodding at his middle area, and his gloved hand automatically shoots down to his trousers.

'Nice one, sir,' he smiles.

The interior of the car looks like it is the length of a football pitch. I'm tempted to lie down on the carpet just to get my money's worth.

'Help yourself to drinks,' says Parker through the intercom, 'and there is a television to your left, madam, if you wish to watch it.'

Mandy makes herself comfortable, sliding her bottom around the leather seats. She's looking out of the blacked-out windows wishing, I expect, that everyone else on the estate could see in. A football kicked by one of the estate urchins hits the side of the car and I slide the electric window down and tell the little fucker to piss off.

'I know your mum and dad and I'll be telling them!' I shout.

'Bollocks!' comes the shouted reply.

His mates run up and squash their faces against the glass to peer in, leaving smudges of snot and greasy fingermarks on the window.

'Put your foot down, mate,' I urge. 'Let's get out of this shit-hole.'

We drive through the streets of south London and cruise over Battersea Bridge and out on to the King's Road, where the limo hardly warrants a second glance. Only fifteen minutes now till we get to the Hilton, I tell Mandy. These Chelsea residents probably think there is a pop band in the back, or even a Hollywood star. They'd be shocked if they knew it was Mr and Mrs King on the way to the Thug of the Year Awards. Well, we were just plain Mr and Mrs King up until I had a book come out and it sold twenty million copies and was translated into fifty languages. Suddenly I was on television, radio and in the papers. Melvyn Bragg did a *South Bank Show* on me and my book-signing tour across England brought whole cities to a standstill. The *Sun* dubbed it 'Bootlemania'. Tony Blair, never one to miss a photo opportunity, was seen at Prime Minister's Question Time with *Hoolifan* poking out the top of his suit pocket. It only really sank in that I had arrived, though, when *Hello!* magazine outbid *OK!* to do a photo shoot of our home.

They turned up unexpectedly one Friday morning. I was sprawled on the settee watching the *Teletubbies* when the doorbell went. Standing on the landing were a man and a woman, dishevelled and both gasping for breath.

'We've just walked up twenty-two flights of stairs,' puffed the woman. The man had both arms against the wall and was hanging his head as he gulped in air. Droplets of his sweat fell on to the concrete.

'Lift broken?'

'We're from *Hello!* magazine,' the woman went on.

'Hello,' I replied.

'Yes, that's right, *Hello!*,' she said.

'No, I meant hello, you know, hello as in hi.'

'I see. I'm sorry.'

'That's *OK!*' I laughed, but she didn't or wouldn't take the bait. The man was starting to recover and was looking at me like I was a bit thick or something. Mandy had obviously heard the exchange because I could hear her scurrying around behind me and revving up the Hoover. I invited them in and offered them a mug of tea.

'Do you mind if I just sit down for a minute?' asked the man as he unloaded his camera gear on to the kitchen table next to the car battery of Mandy's Mini Metro which I had been cleaning up for her the night before.

'This is a surprise. I didn't know you were coming today.'

'Oh yes, we spoke to your wife yesterday.'

Well, she could have told me, I thought. 'Excuse me. I'll just go and get some trousers on.' I'd forgotten that I'd been watching TV in just my boxer shorts. Mandy walked in and almost curtseyed.

'Sorry if we are a bit early,' said the woman.

'Oh no, don't worry,' lied Mandy. 'It's not a problem. To be honest, it completely slipped my mind. Now I expect you'd like a nice cup of tea.'

With one eye on the kitchen table and the dripping battery, they both declined.

'Something stiffer?' suggested Mandy, who still had the ouzo left over from our Corfu holiday in '83. Something stiff like my cock, I'm thinking to myself as I home in on the cleavage on display as the girl bends down and takes her notebook from her bag. I start imagining myself unloading the contents of my sack over her breasts, which are like two puppies fighting to burst out of her bra. Looking at her tanned legs, too, I start getting the popcorn. I wonder if they would agree to some photos of her sitting on my face.

'Which room would you like to begin with?' Mandy enquires and she leads them into the bedroom. She notices the bloke looking a bit queer at the rabbit hutch beside the bed.

'Actually, it's not a rabbit in there,' she explains. 'It's our son's ferret. Don't try and stroke it, he's a vicious bastard. He'll have your finger off before you can say "ouch".'

They took a few snaps of Mandy and me holding hands sitting on the bed and then asked if they could move into the sitting-room.

'Nice-looking fish. What are they?' asked the man as he spotted our four-foot aquarium. He walked over and stirred the water with his finger.

'Piranhas.'

Water splashed on to the dirt-coloured shagpile as he removed his hand at a rate of knots and had a quick glance to make sure his digits were still intact. This time they wanted us on the settee, me with my arm around Mandy. I chucked the boy's Buzz Lightyear out of the way but I must have hit Andtrap because he let out a little grunt.

'What's that?' asked the man, looking quizzically over at

the balcony. I pulled back the curtain to reveal my daughter's Shetland pony, last year's birthday present.

'You can't keep a pony twenty-two floors up in the air. Can you?' The woman seemed genuinely shocked. Don't know why – I'd seen Kenny Jones, the old The Who drummer, in *Hello!* once and he had dozens of horses.

'Well, you know how it is. The kids set their hearts on these pets and then they soon get fed up. We figured the novelty would wear off and we could just let it go, but we've all got quite attached to old Andtrap.'

'What about the smell?'

'It doesn't seem to bother him.'

They didn't seem too worried about taking any more snaps. They gathered their equipment, thanked us and left for the trek down the stairs.

'Thank fuck they've gone,' I sighed, as Mandy shut the door. 'It's hard work being on your best behaviour for those toffee-nosed bastards. Still, the fifty grand will come in well handy. Put the kettle on, girl, I could murder a cup of tea – all that minding me Ps and Qs has left me mouth as dry as an Arab's arsehole.'

Mandy has barely put the fourth sugar in my tea when the bell rings again. It is the *Hello!* people again.

'Can we use the phone please? Our car has been jacked up on bricks outside and the wheels removed.'

Mandy and I shake our heads. Kids these days . . .

The limo turns into Park Lane and pulls up outside the Hilton. In front is another stretch job and I notice the window go down and a pudgy hand throw out a burger wrapper, followed by a fried chicken container and then finally a lemonade bottle. Fucking litter louts, I think, but, to my surprise, out of the car steps Martin Knight and his wife Val. We get out too. A big banner hangs from the entrance, declaring, 'Welcome to the Thug of the Year

Awards 1999.' The press break through the rope cordons and we almost get crushed as well as blinded by the flashing lights. Thank God for the Old Bill, who do a marvellous job restraining these animals.

'Martin, Martin, look this way,' they urge.

'Give us a quote, Martin.'

I feel like saying 'bollocks' but I'm conscious these days of my image and I don't want to spoil it.

'Mandy, can you give Martin a peck on the cheek?' asks one of the photographers.

'You're joking! I'm not dropping me strides in this weather.'

Mandy digs me in the ribs. Then I see Pat, who I used to go to Chelsea with a few years ago. Since launching his *Thug Monthly* magazine, he's gone from strength to strength. His Saturday lunchtime show on L!ve TV, which shows all the best rucks from the previous weekend, has propelled that TV station into the mainstream. They just did a deal with Sky to buy all their out-takes of crowd scenes and they were away.

'What do you think, Mart, about this new law going through Parliament?' he says. A geezer from a German television station brandishing a microphone asks me the same thing. There has been a fuss among the chattering classes recently saying that people fighting at football matches should be compelled to wear protective garments like safety helmets, knee pads, elbow pads and gloves. Of course, I don't agree with this latest attempt to sanitise our national pastime, but I'm not going to let anyone from the media catch me out.

'No comment.'

There are a couple of thousand people cheering, waving scarves and banners and calling my name from behind the crush barriers. One thing Mandy and I have decided is that we will not forget our roots, so I make a point of going over and shaking a few hands. Mums lift their babies aloft and I kiss them. Someone lifts Gregor up and I shake his hand. Martin and Val have filed inside now, so Mand and I wave to the crowd and then turn and walk through the entrance.

'Now I know how Charles and Di felt,' comments Mandy.

'Just think, not so long ago, people would have frowned upon a do like this.' I shake my head as I ponder on the fickleness of public opinion. In the lobby, Martin and Val are chatting to the Duke of Edinburgh but Prince Charles sees me and rushes over. He thanks me for taking his boys, William and Harry, to the recent Chelsea versus Millwall game.

'They really enjoyed it,' he enthused. 'They're forever playing fighting now, saying one is Millwall and one is Chelsea. At Balmoral last week Harry was holding one wing and it was William's job to take it. It did make me chuckle. But really I am very grateful – I am a great believer that one should experience as much as one can.'

'Thanks, Chas. Very nice of you. You having a shant later?'

We agree to meet at the bar afterwards to get lashed up.

'Don't call him Chas,' chides Mandy. 'He's the Prince of Wales.'

'Nah, he doesn't like all that "Your Royal Highness" shit – he told me.'

'Well, you give him a bell in the week and make sure you ain't offended him.'

We are shown to our table which tonight we are sharing with Martin and Val and John King and his girlfriend, Anita.

'I see the Brimsons are here,' says Martin, pointing over to the other side of the ballroom, 'and don't they look smart in their red dickey bows and red waistcoats!'

'All the waiters are wearing them,' I point out.

Mandy must be hungry because she starts tucking the serviette into the collar of her blouse, but then she notices a telegram standing up against the glass in the centre of the table.

'Ah, that's nice. There's a telegram here from Bill, wishing you all the best for tonight.'

'What, Bill from Dagenham or Wild Bill?'

'No, Bill Clinton. It's signed Bill, Hillary and Chelsea.'

The waiter delivers three pints of Guinness for the girls but Martin, John and I wade straight into the bubbly. Rumour has it that Martin and I are up for an award for our book *Hoolifan: Thirty Years of Hurt*, which has massively outsold *Fidget Jones's Dairy* (the hugely successful book about a nervous Welsh schoolkid who becomes Europe's most prosperous dairy farmer) and *Fever Pitch* combined. They're even making it into an opera, with Pavarotti playing the part of Martin Knight.

The Master of Ceremonies calls everyone to order. I whisper to Mandy that these awards are being shown live in over thirty countries. He talks about how, years ago, football rucking was unacceptable and even says that there were people in this hall who had publicly condemned it. There was no room in our national game for violence, they had said. Hang your heads in shame, booms the MC. Jimmy Hill, also wearing a garish bow tie, looks down at his brown Hush Puppies. The MC lightens up and introduces Julian Clary to present the prizes. A huge cheer goes up and develops into a standing ovation. Julian has recently been exposed by a Sunday tabloid as in fact being straight, and this is the audience's way of saying, 'Look we don't care about your sexual orientation. We like you for what you are.'

The first award is for Best Mob and clips are shown on the big screen of the nominees: Chelsea, West Ham, Millwall and Watford. Julian wrestles with the envelope and in his natural Arthur Mullard voice announces that Watford are the winners for their recent row with Barnet.

'I don't fucking believe it!' I fume. 'How did they win that?'

One of the Brothers Grimm holds his Scarrott aloft as the other screams in the microphone about his hatred of L*t*n.

'Get off, you fucking knobheads,' shouts Trevor Brooking from one of the front tables.

I'm pleased about the next award, which goes to my old mate Glen for his hooligan/cookery programme *Can't Fight, Won't Fight*, but his acceptance speech threatens to send everyone to sleep. Eventually Julian shoves him off the stage.

'Now for the Book of the Year award.' The cameras swing around and point over to our table. This must be the worst-kept secret in the world. Martin and I try to look like we don't know we're going to win.

'And the winner is . . . *Wilf Wednesday: The Best Footballer You've Never Even Heard Of*, by Pablo Blewitt.'

We are stunned.

'What the fuck is that?' I ask Martin and John.

'It's all about a Dulwich Hamlet player from the '70s who was a bit of a maverick. Used to like beer and sex and didn't wash his hands after a shit. He caused a storm when Dulwich won the Blake's Incontinence Pants Cup in '78 and he turned up at the victory dinner at the town hall in a Dennis the Menace and Gnasher T-shirt.'

I can't take this. I throw my serviette down in disgust, stand on my chair and shout across the room that the awards are rigged. Martin, John and the girls pretend they are picking stuff up off the floor. But I'm not having it. I throw a half-eaten pig's trotter up on to the stage and kick the chair away from underneath Colin Moynihan, one of the judges, who is sitting on top of a pile of cushions in front of me. The police start pouring in through the double doors and rugby-tackle me to the floor. A policewoman kneels on my chest and starts slapping my face.

'Get up, Martin, get up,' she says.

'Fuck off and leave me alone!' I try to shout.

She starts twisting my ear lobes and then her hand goes down to my groin and gives my nuts a tight squeeze. I look up at her, close my eyes and then open them again. It's Mandy blinking down at me.

'Martin, you've been dreaming. What's the matter? You've had a nightmare.'

ONE

Ten Mad Minutes

> 'Soccer violence has not gone away. It is still very much alive, yet hooligans and policemen are finding that it does not make news anymore . . . Late that night Leeds fans attacked the Jazz Café, a fashionable live-music venue and nightclub, rampaging around the area and attacking bystanders. When they failed to batter down the door of the club with a ripped-out street sign, they turned on clubgoers waiting in the queue. Result: Hooligans 1, Column inches 0.'
>
> John Duncan, *The Guardian*, 12 April 1996

As I walk out of Victoria station, I screw my eyes up as the sunlight hits me in the face. A manky *Big Issue* vendor gingerly steps into my path.

'*Big Issue*? *Big Issue*, guv?' The smell and taste of stale cigarettes, cheap wine and whippet piss hits the back of my throat. Yeah, I really am going to buy your shit magazine, pal. I sidestep him and send up a small flock of pigeons. Like the *Big Issue* dosser, they're in my face as they flap away. I try and toe-punt one up the arse, with no success. How many times have I done that? Launch one but at the last split second they suck their arses in a couple of inches and my well-aimed kick skims thin air.

'Hurry up, you wanker.' There is no mistaking that booming voice. My mate Ally. He's standing at our pre-arranged meet beneath the clock tower opposite the station. There is no mistaking his look either. Like a cross between Terry Waite and Brutus from the *Popeye* cartoons. One big fucker.

'Where the fuck you been, Kingy?'

'How about "Good morning. How are you, Martin?"?'

'Bollocks. You're late as usual.'

'Late! I never finished work till midnight.'

Ally looks at me in that you-are-not-getting-any-sympathy-from-me kind of way and says that none of the others are in the Duke of York as planned. The guvnor has told Ally that the police had instructed him to close on account of information that the Spurs mob planned to meet in there. I suppose if we knew that was where Spurs were meeting then there was a good chance the Old Bill would know too.

Up the road from the York is the Stag and, sure enough, we spot Mark, Muscles and the rest of our boys grouped around the end of the bar. An over-friendly Aussie barman supplies the first lager and I clock another group of geezers, unmistakably football boys, at the opposite end of the bar looking down at us. Ally sees me looking at them looking at us. One of them nods and Ally nods back.

'They're Tottenham,' he announces.

Now Ally is a Spurs fan by birth and all that but he comes to football with us. He's our mate, everyone knows he's Tottenham, but he likes our firm and we like him. He's done it for us and with us time and time again so we know where his ultimate loyalty lies. Ally is also a first. The first of Tottenham's firm that I have socialised with. The only one. I've got every respect for all the other London mobs but Spurs are pond life. Don't abide by the rules. For example, one of their top boys is a convicted child molester and rapist. That says it all. How can any self-respecting firm have a man with such a pedigree as a key member? An ethical code has evolved now. No violence with non-willing partners. Roughly equal numbers at all times. No grassing. No nonces. Spurs cannot be relied upon to abide by the code. But looks like things may be about to change as far as them coming looking for us goes. One of the boys from the far corner walks confidently over and engages Ally and me in conversation.

'All right boys?' Quiet for a minute until Ally replies, 'Yes.' 'Heard about today?' continues the Yid in a confiding tone. 'Well, we're all up from Chichester, us lot. My mate over there,' he points over to a half-wit-looking div, 'recognised you from Spurs. Well, we're off in a minute to Earls Court. Everyone's meeting there and then we're going down the back doubles to do a Chelsea pub. Batter the Chelsea scum in their own backyard.'

You and your mates couldn't batter a fucking cod, we're thinking, but we're all ears. He is still a teenager, this kid. All ginger hair, acne and a brace on his yellow teeth. He's in overdrive now, looking at Ally like he's in the presence of greatness. A fucking moron. I wander over and tell Mark and the others, who want to bash this mob now, but I tell them it is a bad idea. They are not worth it and we may be able to glean a bit more information.

I don't really know why I'm here anyway. I should have phoned in sick. I'm certainly not up for a ruck. I've got a bad back. At least, I started off with a bad back, but now I've got a burnt back. I pulled a muscle at work lifting some heavy boxes of freight and my colleague told me he had a sun lamp at home with a heat lamp facility that was magic for easing muscular pain. So in the week I went around to his gaff and lay under the lamp. My mate came in to the room after about thirty minutes, lifted the lamp and looked at my back.

'Martin, you fucking pratt, you've got this on sun lamp, not heat lamp!'

Jumping up, I could see in the mirror that I looked like I'd fallen asleep on a lilo off Tenerife on a hot day in August. As

I bollocked my pal, who was only trying to help, my back and the tops of the cheeks of my arse began to sting like fuck and I dashed for home. I told Mandy about my predicament – by now my back was one massive blister – and she burst out laughing. Always rely on Mandy for sympathy.

'It's not fucking funny,' I snapped, but the tears were rolling down her cheeks. Meanwhile my cheeks felt like they'd been skinned and the arse-bone was exposed. A row today really is out of the question.

'You lot coming then? We're off to Earls Court,' asks Ginger. Ally tells him we'll catch them later and I'm sure we will. 'Hope you're not after the bird behind the bar?' Ginger's jesting with me now. 'I'll be back after the game to give her a portion.' Then he shouts over to the bemused barmaid, 'See ya later, darlin',' and his face breaks into a leering smile. A smile that reveals the remnants of a cheese and pickle roll entwined in the wiring of his brace. This bloke is unbelievable. It crosses my mind he might be in the Football Intelligence Unit. And off they go, the Chichester Barmy Army, oblivious to the fact they have just been paying homage, and revealing their top men's battle tactics, to a tidy Chelsea firm.

Now even Ally wanted to go outside and pay this lot on stupidity grounds alone. I thought it a good time to tell the boys I'd be no good to them today. I lifted up my shirt and showed them the burnt back and arse. No sympathy here either. Just bags of piss-taking.

We mused over what the Spurs boys had had to say. What pub did the real Spurs mob plan to attack? What backstreets would they be passing through? How big would their mob be and did they really have the bottle to carry it through? We headed off to Chelsea, met up with some more of our boys and told them about the informative encounter with the Yids. We all considered getting off at Earls Court and hunting for the Spurs mob but decided against it. If you followed up every football rumour, you'd end up going up your own arse – in my case, my own burnt arse. Also the police had been evident at Victoria and would probably have followed the little lot we met to their rendezvous, so the ruse would most likely have been tumbled by now. Even if they had shaken off the Old Bill, if a mob of strange faces turns up in a pub within a five-mile radius of the ground, you can be sure the publican will be belling the boys in blue before they are all through the door.

Now we are in the Rose. The pubs we drink in around the ground change frequently. In the early days we used the White Hart but over the last twenty years the Wheatsheaf, the Imperial, the Adelaide, the Black Bull, the Gunter, the Ifield and others have all been in and out of fashion. In come five or six lads telling all and sundry about fifty Tottenham plotted up in an Earls Court pub planning to come down to the ground and turn over one of our boozers. Where did that rumour come from, I wonder? Halfway through the second pint another band arrives, babbling excitedly about the two hundred Yids drinking at Earls Court. Before the third pint was downed the number had swelled to five hundred, and so on. Such is the football grapevine. It certainly was not going to be this boozer that Tottenham would ambush. To get here they would have to pass at least five other pubs heaving with Chelsea, even if they did have the street knowledge to negotiate the Fulham backstreets.

And today of all days there would be more nutters around than usual on account of London derbies drawing out the most psychopathic among the pool of available males. The famous minority that the media tells us about. I remember when I was a kid sitting with the old man on the lower steps of the Shed, whiling away the time before the game started. A fight would break out in the opposite end as the North Stand boys launched their customary attack on the visiting supporters. All around us men and women would jump up clutching their thermos flasks and craning their necks to watch the swaying crowd. 'Go on you Blue boys, give 'em hell!' they'd shout. Then, when the inevitable randomly selected few were ejected from the North Stand end, these middle-aged and elderly people all across the ground would clap them all the way out of the stadium. These were the majority that we, the minority, were ruining the game for.

I remember too Jimmy Hill acting all indignant on *Match of the Day* one Saturday night. Chelsea had played Palace at the Bridge and the match had been punctuated by continued fighting on the terraces. One Chelsea boy had delivered a kung-fu kick that Bruce Lee would have been proud of and the bearded wonder almost creamed his pants. After replaying the kick more times than Willie Carr's famous overhead goal, he made a *Crimewatch*-style appeal. 'Some of you watching now know who these people are. They may be your children; they may be your neighbour's children. Whatever, I implore you to turn them over to the police.' Jim forgot to add 'before my cosy little number is jeopardised any further'. Of course, things have moved on a little now; he'd stand more chance these days interrupting children's programmes and appealing to the little darlings to turn their parents in.

'Let's get out of here,' I suggested as the numbers in the pub made it impossible to get back to the bar for a drink. We decided to find a boozer a little further away from the ground.

'Not too far, though,' said Mark. 'You never know, the Yids might get brave and make a show.'

'No chance,' snorted Craig.

We walked up the King's Road, past the stadium, until we reached the Gunter Arms on the Fulham Road. This too was bursting.

'Fuck it,' said Mark resignedly. 'We'll have to go down the Ifield.'

The Ifield was a quiet little pub tucked away in a Fulham backstreet surrounded by three-storey Victorian dwellings once populated by three poor local families per house, now owned by Rogers and Lucindas galore. It is fabled that it was in here that the original Chelsea boys like Greenaway, Eccles, the Webbs, Jesus and Premo stood around a piano and practised the latest Chelsea songs. Greenaway, they say, was a dishevelled André Previn, working on a piece at home in the bath and then presenting it to the boys for further refinement. I can imagine them all, Boxing Day morning, huddled around the Joanna in their Christmas-present woolly polo necks, singing adapted carols, Eccles passing around small glasses of Dubonnet for refreshment between songs.

Today the pub's half empty but that means we can have a game of pool and a leisurely pint. Potters Bar Dave gets bored watching us trying to emulate Maltese Joe and goes off on a walkabout. Soon he comes back with a bunch of our lot swelling our ranks to about thirty and then he scouts out again. Did Dave have a premonition? He's back, anyway, with a few more and soon this pub too is quite busy. We move outside on this warm day and stand among the Saabs drinking our lager. Dave staggers around the corner, sweating profusely and panting for breath.

'They're coming! They're coming!' he splutters. He bends over, his hands on his knees and his head hanging down by his waist. They, whoever they are, may well be coming but I'm more worried that mouth-to-mouth resuscitation might be required on Dave and the thought fills me with dread. See, Dave is about eighteen stone overweight and is not the fittest of geezers. Yet not that long back he was in tiptop condition after having served in the US Navy for seven years. The best time of his life, he maintains.

'The Yids . . . a good hundred . . . up the road and they've emptied a skip . . . they've got plenty of ammo.' They certainly have, because they appear in front of us and stop momentarily about fifty yards away. Then they charge, making as much noise as possible and giving us the full contents of the skip at a hundred miles an hour. Bricks, bottles, lumps of wood, discarded Habitat bedside lamps – you name it – rain down on us. A brick smacks me on the head and I instinctively feel for blood but there is none. A Spurs fan jumps in front of me in a crouching position. He is wearing swimming goggles and is brandishing a plastic bottle. I think of Billy the Cat, a strip cartoon from the *Beano* comic. The smell tells me that the bottle contains ammonia. You can tell ammonia, not just by the strong odour but because when it hits your clothing it turns a pinky colour. This is typical fucking Tottenham. Can't have a straightener. Got to get tooled up. Catwoman looks at me and squirts at my face. Luckily for me a few drops leak out and drop harmlessly on to the pavement. Stepping forward, I crack the wanker so hard on the jaw that his swimming goggles ride up his head and he falls into a floor of broken glass which shortly before had been one of the Ifield windows.

Some other geezer swings a six-foot plank of wood at my legs and I don't move fast enough. The timber smashes into my shins and I retreat in agony to the pub doorway, where, at least, he cannot use the wood on me. I can weigh up the situation a bit now. The original barrage has forced most of the Chelsea back in to the pub and Tottenham are having a bit of fun with the few of us left outside. But those that are are going at it hammer and tongs and I can see the Spurs boys don't like this. The ammunition is being used up fast and Chelsea are now appearing out of a side door to even up the odds. Spurs step backwards, then turn and walk quickly, and then break into a canter. Ally and I follow but not before a pool ball, chucked by a Spurs boy, hits Ally on the shin. He rolls up his trouser leg to have a gander at any damage and the man with the wood appears and smacks Ally clean around the side of the swede.

'You twot!' growls Ally. 'I'm one of you.' The bloke, clocking the size of Ally and registering the fact that the blow with the wood hadn't put him down, cacks himself. He drops the plank and runs off. In his blind panic he runs between two parked cars and gets himself stuck. Buster Keaton couldn't have bettered it. His face gets splattered all over the back of a nice Volvo estate whilst some of the boys pull at his leg to try and drag him into the road.

Next to this another fracas is taking place over the bonnet of a car. A Yid is trying to parry the efforts of one of ours to stick his face with a broken Budweiser bottle. Somehow, the next thing I know, the bottle is impaled in the back of my hand. Friendly fire, I think they call it. Woodman is down and out, the guy who escaped the Budweiser bullet has scrambled away and Tottenham are now regrouping a hundred yards ahead of us. They walk towards us and we walk towards them. The silence is deafening. Round two, and both mobs are into one another. Fists and boots are flying, and this time no weapons. A good old-fashioned football brawl. How it should be.

The blood was pumping out of my hand and suddenly I felt weak. Then I remembered my back and I felt ill. I stepped back into a doorway and withdrew from hostilities for a minute. The adrenaline of the last ten minutes had made me forget it all but now I was in agony and I slumped back against the wall. Chelsea ran Tottenham back up on to the Fulham Road, where the police (the first we had seen for hours) tidied the situation up.

It was quiet again and I looked around. The scene was unbelievable. The pub looked like the IRA had paid a visit: bricks, mortar, dustbins, wood and piping were strewn across the road, and half a dozen bodies lay motionless. The noise of sirens broke the eerie silence, growing louder and louder.

I hadn't moved for a few minutes when a lone copper came around the corner. 'Are you all right, mate?' The shocked look on his face said it all as he surveyed the carnage.

'I'm okay,' I replied, pulling myself together. 'I just came out of the pub because it was getting a bit smoky and walked into some sort of battle.'

He shook his head incredulously and began to talk into the radio clipped on his lapel. People started to appear sheepishly from the pub and the surrounding houses, looking up and down the road in shocked disbelief at the destruction to the pubs, cars, fences and people.

The fight had gone on for a good ten minutes and by the sound of it hadn't quite finished yet as the police ferried the two mobs up towards the ground. Ally, followed by a convoy of ambulances, appeared from around the corner.

'What happened to yer hand?'

'Some silly bastard stabbed me with a bottle.'

'Fucking Yids!'

'No, Ally, you were standing next to me, it was one of ours that done it. Anyway, how's your leg?'

Ally remembered his leg and rolled up his trousers to have a look. We both started laughing and walked off as the ambulancemen scraped up the bodies, before the police started asking any taxing questions. We turned into the Fulham Road with Ally muttering to himself something about not being able to believe a Yid, one of his own, had tried to do him with a pool ball.

Craig was standing on the corner. 'There's the last of their lot,' he said, pointing over to about twenty Yids heavily surrounded by police. With that, another mob came screaming out of the Gunter and attacked them from behind. The police got among them with horses and dogs and forced the Chelsea back in the pub. We, meanwhile,

carried on walking parallel to the Yids, and there at the front
– I couldn't believe it – was Ginger from the pub in Victoria.
I had to laugh because the wiring in his mouth was all bent
and mangled. He had obviously taken a right-hander in the
boat race, but this didn't stop him giving it the large one.

'You're fucking nothing! Chelsea fucking mugs! We've
taken the piss!' he screamed triumphantly.

'Fuck off!' was the Chelsea reply. 'You're only brave with
Old Bill around yer.'

Someone didn't even care about Old Bill, jumping
through the escort and taking a swipe at Ginger. He was
pounced upon and literally carried away. Ginger persisted.

'We done your fucking pub, Chelsea. We done your
fucking pub.'

He was jumping up and down like a kid having a
tantrum, and then he spotted Ally and me. He went quiet
and winked, then gave a knowing nod. Down by his waist he
was giving us the thumbs up. Silly fucker. He still thought
we were Tottenham. He thought we had infiltrated the
Chelsea mob and he was privileged to be in on the big secret.
Then we passed the Black Bull and the good boys in there
burst out and mullered this rapidly depleting Spurs mob.
Bizarrely, the police were not expecting it – why, I don't
know. If you are going to have to deal with an attack, the
Black Bull is always a likely hot spot. Anyway, they broke
through the police ranks and had Tottenham cowering up
against the wall whilst they kicked fuck out of them. I saw
Ginger getting dragged to the floor and taking a few in the
kidneys and stomach as he crumpled. He was probably
wondering why we weren't helping him. Soppy fucker.

I nipped into the Black Bull to clean my hand up. I had it in
my pocket but the blood was seeping through my jacket. I'd
had to keep my hand well hidden because I'm sure that if the
Old Bill had seen the claret I would have had my collar felt.

They would have put two and two together and made five, even if I had tried to explain that we had been attacked. Looking in the mirror above the washbasin, I could see a lump appearing on the top of my head. I washed my hand and pulled small pieces of glass from the wound. Craig had followed me into the toilets and noticed the bump rising on my bonce.

'That must have been when that Yid hit you with the bottle.'

'What Yid? What bottle?' I asked as I gently dabbed my head with a bit of towel.

'A Yid sneaked up behind and walloped you when you was rucking with a geezer next to a car.'

Well, it was news to me. I never felt it. I was just concentrating on staying upright. If the bastards put you down then, as a rule, that is your lot. Fuck all those wankers who say the best thing is to hit the deck and curl up in a ball. Fuck that – stay standing, where you can see what is going on.

I filed into the West Stand, where all the others were busily talking about the previous hour's events. No one was watching the game. The general consensus was that they couldn't believe the Yids had carried out their threat and come and done a Chelsea pub. I tried to point out it wasn't as simple as that. The Ifield was not where the Chelsea firms drank and Tottenham would have known that. They thought they had picked a soft target and they were unlucky – and we were lucky – that we happened to be in there. Whatever, Spurs will be thinking they've had a right result, even though they got hammered in the end. They made a show deep in Chelsea's territory and you've got to give them credit for that.

At the first-aid post I got a first opinion on my hand and got it cleaned and bandaged. I went back to my seat but told the others I was going to stand in the Shed because my back was giving me real gip. After the game the inevitable rumours started about ambushes and revenge attacks but I was simply not in the mood. All I needed was to get home and collapse in a hot bath. I got all the usual shit about bottling and, when that didn't work, about how they would look after me. Finally it was 'jus' come an' 'ave one drink then'. No way. I boarded a Wimbledon-bound train and the others headed up to Victoria for who knows what. At home I lowered my battered and bruised body into a steaming bath and the day's events swirled around my head. The bump on my head still throbbed as I unfastened the bandage and let my hand fall into the soothing water.

The next morning I awoke positive I'd done fifteen rounds with Mike Tyson. I ached from head to toe. My head from the bottle, my hand from another bottle and my legs from a fucking great lump of four-by-two. I asked Mandy to buy every Sunday paper so I could see what the papers had to say about the trouble. But not a sausage anywhere. Strange, considering there was extensive damage and undoubted casualties. But on Monday the *Evening Standard* devoted their whole back page to the fight. The headline was 'TEN MAD MINUTES' and they had photos of the 'riot' as it was taking place. Apparently on hearing the commotion a local resident grabbed his camera and took thirty-odd pictures of the trouble. The *Standard* published two with the faces of the participants blacked out. The police told the paper that the match had passed peacefully and without incident. A few weeks later, a Chelsea fanzine ran an interview with a high-ranking policeman who claimed that the incident had been blown out of proportion by the newspaper. He argued that it was only a minor skirmish and that his officers had had the situation under control within minutes. About fifteen minutes, I reckon, but then I haven't got a copper's watch.

TWO

The Blunting of the Blades

'There is a diminishing minority who want confrontation but there is a growing group of people who, given the opportunity, will join in. The violence is perhaps increasing but is away from the ground.'

Chief Superintendent Ken Chapman,
The Guardian, 12 April 1996

'Jason Donovan to the window please. Jason Donovan to the window please.' I'm talking over a tannoy at the bloke clearly visible through my plain-glass office window. Still he doesn't move, just continues playing cards. I walk out of the office and stand behind him.

'I'm talking to you, shithead.'

He does not look up but tosses a single card on to the middle of the table. Like cards are his full-time job and me expecting him to carry out any of his baggage-handling duties was an annoying interference.

'I've been calling you.'

Again he ignores me, all his powers of concentration directed at the card school. I feel myself losing it and I kick the chair from beneath him as hard as I can. Jason is thrown off balance and looks up at me as if *I* have acted unreasonably.

'When I call you to the window, you're meant to come to the fucking window.'

'I know,' he replies defensively.

Jason pushes his chair backwards and stands upright facing me. There are forty other men in the room but the only sound now is the Channel 4 racing on the TV. We are eyeball to eyeball for a few seconds but Jason then grabs my hand in both of his and shakes it.

'Sorry, Kingy. I got a bit engrossed in the old poker there.'

'No problem, Jase. Your table's on a meal break so come and see me in forty minutes. I got something to tell you.'

I'd been working at Heathrow, or Thief Row, as it was more aptly called, for two years now and Jason and I had started on the same day. His name was really Stuart but he looked like Jason Donovan of *Neighbours* fame – or how Jason Donovan would look if he lived on liberal portions of lager and curry. We had become good workmates and as he was a Spurs fan I introduced him to Ally, who in turn introduced him to some of the top Spurs boys, which gave him a thrill. All I wanted to tell him was that I had two tickets for the Chelsea versus Sheffield United game today and my boss, being a good old Chelsea boy, had given us the nod to take the afternoon off. How bad was that? The afternoon off and getting paid to watch the football. And he gives me the blank!

To add a bit of spice to the day, I'd heard there was going to be a pre-arranged off before the game. One of Chelsea's faces had got friendly with a couple of Sheffield Wednesday boys through England games. Now Wednesday abhor United with a passion. I would say their hatred runs deeper than that of the two Manchesters, or West Ham and Mill-wall, or even Newcastle and Sunderland. They take it really seriously. Ambushing one another in Sheffield, often when they are not playing each other, is a common occurrence. We've heard about some unbelievable rows between the two groups and it depends on who you're talking to as to who came out on top. I knew the old Wednesday mob and my feeling was that at that time they had the upper hand, but then I was only consorting with them. I hadn't met this new, younger England lot.

These Wednesday boys had rung the Chelsea face and told him where United would be drinking in London before the game. Better still, they gave over the home phone numbers of the main faces at United. These got distributed among Chelsea's mob within hours and before you knew it the telephone lines between London and Sheffield were red hot. By all accounts, the conversations went something like this:

'Hello, lard arse. You down for the game on Saturday?'

'Who is this? How did you get my number?' the startled United fan retorted.

'Don't worry about that, fat bollocks. We've heard you're drinking in Camden before the game. Is that correct?'

'I don't go no more,' blurted out the Yorkshireman. He was probably in a state of shock over the fact that someone from another mob had gone to the trouble of finding his number and calling him at home. A call in the background ended the conversation.

'Come and eat your tea before it gets cold, son.'

These calls continued all week – 'Enjoy your tea, tubs?', 'Ready for Saturday, gutsy?' and so on. The Chelsea boys had no idea what this man's physical build was like but assumed that if he was from Yorkshire he would be a fat bastard. Eventually the old lady grabbed the phone and shouted at the Chelsea lot to leave her boy alone. He had done nothing to them and if he received any more calls she'd be fetching police. The Chelsea boys roared up and started shouting 'Timothy' down the phone, imitating Ronnie Corbett's dominating mother in the TV comedy *Sorry*.

It was one thing giving it the biggun up north but we had the best mob in the country at the time and took this sort of thing very seriously. Chelsea also made up the bulk of the

England mob that had become a powerful magnet to firm members up and down the country. It became a matter of pride for clubs to have representation at international level, as witnessed by the variety of club flags on display at any England game. But it was the Chelsea mob that ran the show and the other clubs deferred to their dedication. The international scene threw up some tabloid stars like Scarrott of Nottingham Forest. The press painted a picture of a fearsome hooligan raping and pillaging his way across the world, draped in a Union Jack. The reality was that he liked a drink and he liked winding up reporters. Most people avoided him.

The United itinerary was relayed by phone across the Chelsea mob. It was important now to be careful with this sort of information. Careless talk in the wrong pub or to the wrong people could mean the Old Bill turning up or, worse still, every wannabe firm member turning up and flooding the event. Chelsea had selected a quiet public house only a mile from where United were set to rendezvous.

I told Jason about what I had heard was going to happen and his face lit up.

'What, we're going to be in a real football row?' he squeaked, like I'd offered him up Kylie Minogue as an escort and the meter had been turned off.

'Hang on, Jase. I thought you was one of the boys down at Tottenham,' I teased.

'Na, not really. This sounds like the business,' he gabbled excitedly whilst doing the Ali shuffle around me and shadow boxing my head. This was like taking a small kid to the circus. I told him that our lot were meeting in the Southampton opposite Mornington Crescent tube station and the Sheffield contingent would be drinking just up the road in the World's End pub. I explained that we would be getting out at Camden because Mornington Crescent tube was shut at the weekend.

'How many d'you reckon they'll bring down?' enquired Jason.

'A couple of thousand, because it's the cup. Also Vinny Jones is playing against one of his old clubs, so that'll pull a few more in. And what with all the winding up on the phones, I reckon Sheffield will be right up for it. They're meant to have a right tasty mob these days.'

Jason had gone very quiet as the prospects on offer dawned on him. The nearer we got to Camden, the quieter and paler he became. Bottle trouble, I think they call it.

Into the daylight, and the pub the United lot were supposed to be meeting in was facing us, dead opposite the tube entrance. It was a normal Saturday morning north London scene. Busy middle-aged women nipping in and out of shops buying their food and household essentials, older couples leisurely shopping together, and solitary men heading for the betting shops for their first study of the day's racing. As is par for the course in north London, the traffic was gridlocked. We squeezed between the bumpers of the stationary cars and peered intently at the pub.

'Dead as a dodo,' I mused. 'Don't look like they've shown. No Old Bill plotted up waiting either.' Jason's face showed relief and disappointment at the same time. We headed off down Camden High Street to the Southampton to see if the Chelsea boys were in there. Coming towards us on the other side of the road were two well-known Chelsea top boys. As they weaved in and out of the traffic, their faces were set in grim determination. They crossed the road and went straight into the pub opposite the station.

'Hold up, Jase. This looks interesting.'

'D'you know those two fellas then?' asked Jason.

'Sure do. And I think they know something we don't.' I felt like a gamekeeper who has taken a tourist on safari and has just spotted two prowling tigers. We leant on the metal railing that ran along the edge of the kerb and waited.

Within seconds they had walked backwards out of the

door on to the street, followed by what we thought was a group of about five or six geezers, but they just kept on coming. The Chelsea pair stepped back slowly to let as many out through the door as wanted to come. They didn't bat an eyelid as the mob surrounded them.

'Stroll on, boys,' grinned the first Chelsea face. 'Two hundred on to two. I don't think so.' He shook his head as if in disbelief that the Sheffield boys would consider such a thing. The Sheffield lot were at a loss as to how to deal with this. The Chelsea boy was well and truly running this confrontation so far.

'Give us a chance to take a little walk down the High Street. You wait here like good boys and we'll be back to beat the fucking granny out the lot of you.'

As he said this, the Chelsea lad directed his words at one particular northerner who was jutting his face forward and holding his arms tense by his side, as if the invisible man was restraining him.

'Fuck off, you Chelsea scum. Let's do it now,' he growled.

Before he could do anything, a big half-caste bloke stepped forward. He looked and acted like he was their top boy. I recognised him from a game a few years previously.

'Let lads go,' he instructed, 'but make sure you come back now.'

Chelsea reconnaissance walked off down the road. I don't know whether they saw the reinforcements trotting towards them or not, because I hadn't, but after fifty yards they stopped, swung around and shouted, 'Come on then, Sheffield, you're right, let's have it now!'

This was all the encouragement this mob needed to take on a firm two strong. But these Chelsea boys had vast experience in unarmed combat and dispatched the first three to reach them with clinical precision. Sheffield stopped dead to re-evaluate the situation, as now sixty-odd of the Chelsea from the Southampton had joined the first two. Sheffield numbers were still around two hundred and they quickly charged again. Again, though, they copped right-handers and they started to hesitate. Really, what did they expect? Two of Chelsea's boys come into their pub to check they are here. The Chelsea pair then take their mob on and don't run. Do they really think they are going to run when sixty of their mates have arrived and are standing shoulder to shoulder?

Some Yorkshiremen sneakily leapt the barrier and walked along the street, trying to melt into the shopping crowd. Loyal firm? I think not.

'Don't fuck off, lads. The fun's just starting!' I said to a couple who looked at us incredulously. They must have wondered just who we were, calmly leaning on the barrier in our airport jackets and ties as fighting raged around us.

Whilst my attention had been momentarily diverted, someone had clumped the big half-caste and he had fallen forward on to the ground. He was sparko, prostrate on the floor, like the Pope kissing the tarmac. His flock was panicking, running every way except forward at the Chelsea.

'Stand! Stand!' went up the cry, which as sure as night follows day heralds a mob that is about to have it on its toes. They paused only to drag their leader away.

'This is better than *Casualty*!' gasped Jason.

'*Crossroads* is better than *Casualty*,' I countered but, judging by the puzzled look on his face, I gathered that he wasn't old enough to remember the riveting soap about a Birmingham motel. Yet again as Sheffield retreated, the numbers difference sank in. Logic and pride told them they should be murdering the Chelsea lot.

'Yes, come on!' they screamed as if they were about to unleash some secret weapon. But there is no freaking this Chelsea firm. I knew almost every single member of the group engaged in this spat and they ran from no one. A cliché, I know. But true. It was a mixture of seasoned football fighters aged between thirty and forty, young guns hungry for the off, and a smattering of London psychos currently following Chelsea because you get a better class of ruck. Numbers didn't bother them. In fact, they preferred to have the odds piled up against them. More sense of achievement.

United ran good and proper this time. Half of them headed down the tube. No doubt searching for a souvenir kiosk to buy their plastic beefeaters to take back to the steel town. Others ran like Linford up the high street and the rest tried to get back in to their pub. Unbelievably, they fought each other to get in the door first. Chelsea followed and tried to enter the pub but United must have barricaded the door with human bodies because it would not budge.

A wooden barstool comes crashing through the big window from the inside and lands on the path. Chelsea momentarily back off and United, sensing a turning point in proceedings, come pouring out. Chelsea are going nowhere even though glasses and bottles and other ammunition gathered from the pub are hurtling in their direction. One Londoner bends down and picks up the stool by one of its legs, swings it around his head like a cowboy with a lasso and then brings it down with vicious force on the nut of a Yorkshireman. Jason and I both wince at the sound of wood on bone. They charge back into the pub, but this time there is no attempt to hold the door as they run for the back exits and vault the bar in an effort to hide out in the living quarters of the staff.

'Good job that window went in,' remarked Jason. 'Now we can see what's happening inside the pub.'

The sound of police and ambulance sirens is clear but they are not getting nearer, presumably jammed up in the traffic. Someone has let off a fire extinguisher in the boozer and people come stumbling out the door covered in white foam. Can't tell who is who now. A solitary policeman finally turns up. Judging by his struggle to capture breath, he has obviously left his vehicle and run through the traffic.

'Come far, officer?' I enquire. He darts me an angry sideways look. In other, less urgent circumstances I think he'd have dug me out. He looks inside the pub and surveys the damage as the last of the attackers disappears into the crowd.

'Did you see what happened?' asks the officer, addressing a crowd of bystanders, including us, who had quite clearly seen everything that had happened.

No reply.

'Did anyone see what happened?' he asks again, wiping the sweat from his brow. A little old lady negotiates her wicker shopping trolley to the front of the crowd.

'I think there has been a fight,' she offers. Everyone sniggers. Even the shocked general public of Camden sees the funny side of this. The copper does not; stupid old bastard, he is thinking. More police turn up on foot and still the sirens wail. If you've got heart problems, remember not to live in Camden. They'll never get you to hospital.

The police usher out the fifty Sheffield fans left in the pub. Many are limping, some are bleeding, and most are covered in white foam. Still none the wiser as to what has happened here, the Old Bill start to take the names and addresses of the Yorkshiremen and make them empty their pockets. As far as they are concerned, they have been fighting amongst themselves.

Police cars and ambulances finally break through and an inspector jumps out and takes control. He susses the situation straight away and tells his officers to abandon name-taking. He tells the ambulancemen to go into the pub and take out those who are still strewn across the carpet. He turns around to the pac-a-mac brigade I'm standing with and tells us to go home and that we have seen enough for one day. Obediently, all the old grunters turn and shuffle off in different directions.

'Fucking Nazis,' mutters one old boy, but I don't know if he is referring to the football crowd or the policemen who have just told him to leave.

'Thought you liked a row at football,' says Jason as the police herd the United fans across the road to the station.

'No, I don't like fighting. Full stop. Even if I did, I'm not going to perform dressed up in the company suit, am I? Remember the induction course, Jase, when we started at the firm? The geezer said if we're collared doing anything untoward in the firm's uniform, that was it – curtains. No final warning. Tin-Tac time.'

We tail the United fans down the escalators and on to the platform. We earwig the conversations. It's inquest time.

'What the fuck was all that about?'

'Why did we run? There was only fifty fucking cockneys.'

'Running from Chelsea! I don't believe it.'

Settling back against the glazed wall, I can't help smiling. This is privilege indeed. To be privy to the confidential discussions of a rival mob. I want to hear every word so I can tell the others. Jason is not so relaxed. He's back in cheek-tightening mode. The northerners are angry, still frightened, and are darting searching glances at everyone. Jase would rather we stood down the other end of the platform.

Directly in front of us, one Sheffield lad is examining his mate's ear. As he turns I can see he has a nasty gash running from beneath his lobe down his neck. His mate asks how it happened.

'Chelsea bastard caught me with a punch. Think he must have been wearing dusters. We should have stood. I'm sure we could have done the bastards.'

'It was them, though. Wasn't it? The Headhunters?' This interjection came from a young, skinny fan whose bottom lip was bruised and swollen.

'That was the Headhunters all right. The fucking age of them! Some of those geezers were forty if they were a day.'

'And that was Icky, weren't it – the geezer with the ponytail?' Lips again, almost hopefully.

'Na, that ain't Icky. He's banged up, he is.'

'No he's not. He runs a youth hostel in Sweden, but that fat bastard at the front, that was the Fatman.'

Yeah, and I'm Captain Mainwaring from *Dad's Army* in my airport uniform, I think to myself. Their fantasies about who had just tonked them seemed to help them deal with the humiliation.

'We ain't been run for three or four years and it was best lads out today. Can't understand what went wrong.'

'Too many people lost their bottle,' volunteers the voice of reason from behind. Couldn't have put it better myself. The voice of reason, though, has also homed in on Jason and me and nudges the bloke next to him. What colour is left in Jason's face drops down his legs to his feet. He asks if we should move down the platform. I feel like jibbing him but he's almost crying anyway. A train arrives and the Sheffield fans scramble on for seats. We stay put. With the doors safely shut, they crowd up against the window and give us the wankers sign and the two-finger salute. Tarts.

Within seconds the next train has pulled in and the Chelsea mob are packed in like sardines. It seems that when the police turned up at the pub, they trotted up to Kentish Town and got the tube there. I inform them that the Sheffield are on the train in front. They smile smiles of satisfaction when I briefly recount their conversations. Jason and I squeeze in and we head towards Stamford Bridge, where we assume the police will take the United lot straight away. Changing at Embankment, we see Tony coming towards us with a bunch of his boys. Some are limping, others have bloody noses and black eyes, all are grinning from ear to ear.

'What happened, Tone?'

Tony's eyes are sparkling despite him finding it difficult to talk through rapidly swelling lips.

'We went off to find another station other than Camden, jumped on the train and then the doors opened and we were back at Camden. And they're all standing on the platform. They get on. The doors shut. No introductions are required. Train pulls out and all hell is let loose. We back ourselves into a corner and give it out as good as we get. Kick for kick. Punch for punch. We've gotta fight. No option. Good thing was, it's such a confined space only about half a dozen of them can get at us at one time. They're fucking brave, those northerners, because there is just the six of us and at least thirty of them. We manage to stay upright until the end, when one goes down. Next station, doors open, and they step backwards off the train. But matey on the deck – they drag him off the train by his feet and he's out. They're kicking fuck out of him and his head hits the platform when they yank him from the train. That seems to wake him up. His shoe comes off and he wriggles free and manages to jump back on the train. United are going ape-shit now. It's this geezer they want and they know him. He's Wednesday's boy and they've tumbled who's been informing us. Anyway, we manage to hold them off and Old Bill turn up. Our friend's had enough. I s'pose he's heading back to Sheffield via a shoe shop.'

Tony can barely finish the story through laughing. For most people, the last half-hour would have been a traumatic experience, but for him it was a real high.

Seems like it's happening all over this day because at the ground I bump into Fat Pat. Well, he was once Fat Pat, but now he's done the weight he's just Pat. He is a great one for recounting funny football stories and is the fount of all knowledge when it comes to football thuggery. Pat has a network of friends all around the country and can tell you within hours how Hartlepool had done Darlington, about Middlesbrough rucking with Cardiff in the cup, how fifty

Oldham ran the main Leeds crew, and that Spurs got mashed by fifty Mancs at Maine Road. If it happened, then Pat knew all about it. He should have been the editor of *Thug Monthly* (now there's a thought) if such a magazine existed. Anyway, Pat tells me he and a few others had run five or six Sheffield geezers up a side street over in north London. When they turned the corner, the United boys had clean disappeared. Pat and company couldn't work out where they had got to – they had not been that far behind. They were checking under cars and behind privet hedges when a little old lady with a shopping trolley approached them.

'Excuse me, boys, but I think who you are looking for are in there.' She pointed over towards the fish and chip shop.

'Thanks luv,' said Pat and they rushed across the road. Sure enough, the United boys were in there trying to act like they were buying fish and chips. But busily shaking a bottle of vinegar into the palm of their empty hands did not fool Pat and the boys. A couple of them managed to vault the counter and escape out the back. A few didn't.

Jason and I stand in the Shed. United are packed in to the North Stand and you've got to give it to them – it's a good show. Indeed, it's rare these days at Stamford Bridge for the opponents to turn up, let alone be up for the ruck. But there is no infiltrating the North Stand now. Years ago a piss-poor mimicking of the accent of that dozy sod off the Wheeltappers and Shunters Club was enough to get you past the Old Bill; now it would be easier to invade Kuwait.

Vinny Jones gets booked shortly after kick-off and the Sheffield fans are calling for his blood. A few weeks ago they would have been cheering him but I doubt whether Vinny will be fazed in any way. Chelsea win the tie and suddenly the optimistic blue faithful are thinking of Wembley. The Sheffield fans are held in until the police deem the streets of Fulham are safe enough for them to begin the long journey back home. For our part, we adjourn to the pub at Charing Cross where we normally meet after home games. Some of our chaps arrive and excitedly tell us that they met up with some Sheffield fans on the train and they had told them they'd be drinking in the West End till late and were definitely up for a straightener. Half of the pub decides to go and find them now among the tourists and drunks in Covent Garden. We stay for a couple more. Within the hour they're back, even more excited than when they left. Apparently they eventually found each other and Sheffield stood and fought. It seems that they narrowly came off worse again in this latest brawl and a couple were left prostrate on the floor when the police turned up.

I must be getting old, me. Because some of these blokes here – my friends – have just had their third serious fight in the space of six hours! I'm not sure I've got the stamina or the hunger for the row as much as I used to. Looking at Jason, he looks like he hasn't slept for six nights. He's shell-shocked. Time to go home.

As we step outside, London is busy. Snakes of black taxis jerk forward, dropping off and collecting people from a hotel. A couple of 'homeless' people and their dogs sit begging on the pavement, waiting to collect enough for another can of Super Tennent's before returning to their houses. Middle-aged couples grandly attired in furs, dinner jackets and bow ties arrive from the suburbs bound for Theatreland. I reflect momentarily on the diversity of London life and how, intertwined in all this, in little pockets of the capital, gangs of men in their twenties, thirties and forties who had never met before and probably would not meet again tried all day to hospitalise each other.

A police carrier heads towards the pub. A dozen faces framed in helmets glare out at me. I know the expression. It is the look of young men about to have a row. They are searching for confrontation but I am not and I stare ahead fixedly and stride past them. As I disappear towards the underground I can hear the sliding and crashing of doors and the clattering of boots as they charge into the pub.

Meanwhile, across London an elderly man screws his pools coupons into a ball and throws it across the sitting-room into the wastepaper bin. He has not had a good day. His Saturday Yankee yielded nothing and he broke his own rule again about not having any other bets. He lost fifteen pounds in total, which was a sizeable chunk of his pension and cash he can ill afford to lose. Noel Edmonds comes on the telly and he feels even more depressed.

He hears the Yale key turning in the door and suddenly his spirits are lifted. Dolly is back from shopping. This means food, a hot drink and a bit of chat to take his mind off this Saturday's financial misfortunes. Dolly parks her shopping trolley in the hall, removes her headscarf and coat, and flattens her hair with her hand as she gives herself the once-over in the mirror before entering the sitting-room.

'You'll never guess what I seen today, Bert love.'

Bert leans forward and switches the television off.

'I've just watched a blinding row between Chelsea and Sheffield United.'

'Who won?'

'Chelsea, of course. And then a bit later on I saw some of those northern yobs run into the chippie and hide, so of course I told those nice Chelsea chaps where they were.'

'Well done, pet – now why don't you make a nice pot of tea and tell me all about it.'

The next time Chelsea and Sheffield United met was in a league game at Stamford Bridge. Again, we heard through our Wednesday contacts that United were up for revenge. The mobile phones of both mobs throbbed for a couple of days until a meet was arranged at Gloucester Road station for two o'clock. Pat informed me that two coaches were expected and that he had even provided them with useful parking information. He added that the Wednesday lads had decided against joining up with us this time. A useful Chelsea firm gathered in a nearby pub and waited. No show by seven o'clock, so I guess United had the last laugh.

THREE

The City United

*'What statistics cannot show is that the oppressive atmos-
phere surrounding a football match no longer exists. It is
not fashionable to parade around in intimidating
groups.'*

Craig Brewin, spokesman for the
Football Supporters' Association,
The Guardian, 10 January 1992

'Sleep well, Trev?'

I bend down and leave Trev a steaming mug of tea next to
the bed. He does not stir but my Dobermann, Bodger, does,
appearing from the opposite end of the quilt and excitedly
giving me an early-morning wash with his big pink tongue.

'Fuck off, you poxy fucking dog,' complains Trev, now
wide awake. But Bodger thinks Trev is sweet-talking him.
'Fucking dog of yours. Kept me up nearly all night. I got
undressed to get into bed, switched the light off and went to
get in but he's on the bed and he starts growling. I get out,
put the light back on and tell him to get off. He does, but
then when I try to get back in he's back on the quilt fucking
snarling again. Then I see he's got one of my socks in his
mouth.'

'I should have told you, Trev. Don't leave your socks lying
around. He loves socks. Anything, really, with a bit of
personal odour. We had Mandy's cousin staying with us for

a while whilst she was training to be an air hostess at Heathrow and one evening we had some friends over for dinner – and Bodger appears in the room, tail stump going nineteen to the dozen, with Mand's cousin's knickers draped over his snout. Another time Jeff was staying and he was on the edge of the bed pulling his socks on when Bodger snatched a sock out of his hand and swallowed it whole! Jeff was gutted. It took a day to pass through his system but was as good as new after a spin in the washing machine – but Jeff didn't want it back.'

'Wonder why?' says Trevor and goes on to tell me how he ended up sharing the bed with Bodger and although he tried to sleep he could feel Bodger's eyes staring at him. Every time Trev opened his eyes, sure enough, all he could see were the whites of the dog's eyes in the darkness.

The reason why Trev was staying with me was that we were off to Manchester to see the City versus United derby. It was one of the games I'd always fancied going to. Like Barcelona/Real Madrid, Rangers/Celtic or Inter Milan/AC Milan, it was a clash with a bit of edge to it. I'd done all the London derbies and now my curiosity was taking me further afield. Trev's a Millwall fan and when I mentioned that a mate of mine was getting some tickets he asked to be included in the expedition. This would be a novelty for him, watching a real match with the odd fight breaking out instead of the usual diet down at Millwall – a real fight with the odd bit of football thrown in.

The din of my two other Dobermans going berserk in the garden heralded the arrival of Dave, who was driving us northwards today. We wolfed down the fry-up that Mandy, darling that she is, had rustled up for us at this early hour and set off to collect Dave's mate Mike. These two had met whilst serving in the US Navy, first coming across each other on a naval base in the States. Dave was a chef on submarines, whilst Mike did the same job on an aircraft carrier, and they had both joined the US forces on the grounds that their fathers were US nationals.

One day Dave was serving a queue of ravenous marines when one mentioned to him that there was another Limey, who was also a chef, on another part of the base and that this other fella was from a place called Manchester. Dave told the marine that the next time he saw the Manchester Limey he should ask him why it is that Manchester United always run from Chelsea. The marine didn't really understand so Dave went on to explain the rivalries between the supporters of the various English football teams and how some fans were better at fighting than others. 'Sure, but why do they wanna fight in the first place?' I don't know how Dave answered that one but he filled the fascinated Yank in on the full history of the Chelsea/United battles. A few days later, the marine was waiting for Mike to slap a scoop of veg on his plate when he leant forward and stared into Mike's eyes.

'How come United always run from Chelsea?'

'Pardon?'

'You heard. Why do you Mancs always shit out and why not admit that Chelsea once cleared the Stretford End?'

'Who you been talking to?' asked a bemused Mike and then the marine told him about Dave on the other side of the base. The two eventually met up, had a good laugh over the wind-up and became friends. When they left the navy, Mike came to Chelsea and for a time probably spent more time with us than at United games. He was always telling us that the United/City derby was the ultimate row so today we have decided to see for ourselves.

We picked Mike up at Hitchin, where he was now living, and got on to the A1. On the journey, all we spoke of was rowing, Dave and I recounting various Chelsea head-to-heads and Mike telling us all about the Red Army and their exploits. We knew we'd reached the bullshit zone when Trev started fantasising about Millwall winning the European Cup.

Arriving in Manchester around midday, we parked up and found a pub very close to the ground. Even at this time it was packed. The first thing I noticed was the range of dialects bouncing around the bar: Irish, West Country, Welsh, Nordic and Swahili. People from all over the world seemed to have congregated here to watch United play – every corner of the globe, it seems, except Manchester. Mike explained that Manchester people follow City and that United draw their support from all over.

Through one of those quirks of childhood, in a way I followed City. After Chelsea and Millwall I always look for their result. One birthday my mum and dad bought me a Subbuteo table-football game. Subbuteo was all the rage for a while and the manufacturers must have sold lorry loads for years. All the kids had it and unlike blow football and other predecessors this was the business. Everyone took it really seriously. At its basic level it consisted of a green felt pitch you flattened out on the carpet and teams of miniature plastic players that were flicked around with a ball almost the same size as the footballers. I was thrilled as I smoothed out the pitch on to a bumpy carpet and crawled around on my hands and knees setting the goals up. I opened up the first of the green rectangular boxes that contained the teams that Mum had bought me and it was Manchester City in their light-blue shirts. The other box was Tottenham.

'Thought you'd like Chelsea and Spurs for starters,' she smiled.

Around the same time, Manchester City made the FA Cup final and beat Leicester 1–0, although ironically they played in red and black striped shirts to avert a colour clash with Leicester. The game was not a brilliant one but the team caught my imagination, Joe Mercer and Malcom Allison – the wise old man and the maverick – running the show, the likes of the dependable but creative Colin Bell in midfield and Mike Summerbee weaving a bit of magic on the wing, with Francis Lee bustling around the penalty area waiting to strike. They were normally the underdog to the universally loved Manchester United club, but at this time they rose up and overshadowed their neighbours.

I soon added the real Chelsea team to my collection of Subbuteo teams, as well as many others. I also bought floodlights, referees, grandstands and corner flags and my mates would come round for hours and play intense and competitive tournaments. A boy who lived nearby who was a Man United fanatic even used to paint his players so you could identify individuals. Using Airfix model paint, he painted one's head skin colour for Bobby Charlton, added long black hair and a beard to another for George Best and gave long blond locks to John Fitzpatrick. But for Mum the novelty wore off fairly early on. She was forever walking across the pitch on her way to the next room, crushing Joe Corrigan or Charlie Cooke in the process, and when I complained, she would go into one.

'Take yer mates and yer stupid fucking game around their houses and see if their bleeding mums like it! I'm trying to do my housework and I've got you and this lot under me feet.' Before long I was playing with twenty-two bases and no players as they perished under Mum's slippers or up the Hoover.

We leave the pub and slip into one of the many takeaways that pepper Old Trafford's immediate surroundings. Mushy peas with everything seems to be the order of the day. Not for me; reminds me too much of *The Exorcist*. We stand and eat our tucker on the forecourt outside the club shop, where, Mike informs us, the top United faces meet.

'Last time I was here we had a right old battle with Leeds – right on this very spot.'

He's coming across like some old rustic tour guide pointing out where King Harold fell at the Battle of Hastings.

'Yeah, they turned up at ten to three, about a hundred and fifty of them. If Old Bill hadn't turned up we'd have murdered them.'

All around, an endless stream of coaches empty their red-faced loads right next to where we are standing. Ted Tingle's Luxury Travel, Dorset, reads one; another is O'Shea's of Limerick, which has an Irish tricolour flag with the word 'United' painted on it hanging from the rear window. Now I thought Chelsea had some pull with swathes of support across Surrey, Sussex, Kent, Berkshire and Essex, but the range of Manchester United is something else. How anyone knows anyone is beyond me. Mind you, I can remember that back in the '70s Chelsea had a little firm that came up, especially to away games, from Exeter, and other bigger mobs that were Bolton- and Birmingham-based used to appear from time to time.

The buzz sweeps around the forecourt that the first City firm has been sighted. A big black man with dreadlocks is announcing the same thing time and time again like a town crier: 'They're meeting in a pub in Moss Side and they're heading this way.' Well, I could have told him that! Speculation then takes over. They are in a pub in the city centre and they are going to arrive dead on kick-off seems to be the new consensus. A fella ambles over and shakes Mike by the hand and he in turn introduces Dave, Trevor and me.

'What's occurring?' asks Mike eagerly, like this geezer will be the one who really does know.

'City met at eleven this morning over at Cheadle.'

Dave, Trev and I look at one another and, although we try not to, start laughing. It was the name Cheadle that did it. Northern towns have got such stupid fucking names that it is difficult to take mention of them seriously. The geezer explains in his best geography-teacher voice that Cheadle is on the other side of Manchester.

'Well, that's three different places they've been in in the last five minutes,' I comment.

By now the numbers on the forecourt have grown to a few hundred but I wonder how many of this lot are the rucking type. Not a lot, I conclude. I fancy most of them would fuck off at the first sign of a rival gang. They certainly are not well organised or well prepared and I reckon Chelsea, Spurs, West Ham or Millwall would go straight through them like a knife through butter. Only the big black ticket touts look like they are capable of holding their hands up, but they are too busy knocking out tickets at sixty pounds a throw to gormless overseas fans draped in scarves and wearing silly hats.

'City scumbags at the crossroads!'

The shout goes up and the forecourt empties as one and heads up the road to the junction.

'I've got to see this,' I laugh to Trev as we follow the hordes.

'I thought you'd seen it all, Mart.'

'Na, this could be a first. Seeing City coming towards us rather than the backs of their heads as they run off as fast as their legs will take 'em.'

At the crossroads it's handbags at thirty paces, with the police firmly implanted in the middle of the two mobs. City are ushered into the stadium whilst United indulge in some mutual back-slapping. Like they've achieved something. This will be something to tell their mates in the pubs of Dorset and County Wexford tonight.

On entering the ground we take up our seats in the Scoreboard End, at the opposite end of the arena to the world-famous Stretford End. The atmosphere is half carnival, half riot bubbling under. Manchester City are immediately below us and at this point are making more noise and come over as more volatile than the home supporters. Mind you, as we have already ascertained, the truth is that City *are* the home supporters.

Today's game is the first time the two clubs have met since the so-called Battle of Maine Road, when a couple of hundred United fans, Mike included, were chased out of the Kippax, City's end. United ran on to the pitch and were laughed and jeered back into their own enclosure. According to Mike, the whole day was highly embarrassing and the United mob were out for revenge today. Judging by the posturing outside, my money was saying they would not be getting it.

The match begins at the usual frenetic pace that characterises local derbies but soon City score a magnificent goal. I almost jump up and punch the air but all around is a gasping silence, as if each member of the crowd has been simultaneously thumped in the stomach. But below, City are going berserk, jumping into each other's arms and into the air. A few growlers in our area stand up and scan the United seats for a smile, a stifled cheer – any giveaway that a stray City supporter is in their midst.

The goal transports me back to 1974, when Denis Law back-heeled a ball to score and send United into the old second division for the first time in living memory, the irony being that Denis Law, along with Charlton and Best, was a United icon whom they had offloaded to their neighbours when they decided he was past his best. It is also remembered because those were the days when *Match of the Day* didn't skirt around any disturbances on the terraces. Around the same time, Jimmy Hill gave a blow-by-blow account of a good old pitch fight between Derby County and Chelsea at the Baseball Ground. After Denis's goal, United fans invaded the pitch and did their best to get the game abandoned. However, everyone knew this was too good an opportunity to waste and the game was eventually completed. Grown men broke down and cried at the prospect of visiting York,

Shrewsbury, Grimsby and Walsall. United's glory days were over (for a short time anyway) and the rest of the country, except poor old Denis Law, loved it.

This game ends in a draw – another predictable aspect of derbies – and we slowly wind our way on to the stairs and over to the exits. A voice comes booming across the emptying seats.

'Kingy! Oi, Kingy, you Chelsea no-good wanker!'

Jimmy O'Neill, a Cockney Red from south London, is clambering across the rows to approach me. He pumps my hand.

'What you doing here?'

'Same as you, Jim – watching football.'

I get the introductions out of the way and we talk about old times. Tooting and Mitcham's cup run in the '70s crops up.

'I'm meeting Banana Bob and Griffin outside, if you fancy a drink,' Jim says.

I decline the offer and Jim goes on his way. Mike wonders how I know Jim and says he is a big face at United.

Back on the forecourt, evening sports papers are already on sale. The game's only been finished half an hour and here is the match report blazed across the front page. No such service at Chelsea. Not even London! There we are, the capital city, and we cannot rustle up an evening paper on a Saturday any more. Mind you, everything about United is different class. It is obvious that there is a new attitude here towards the fans. They are treated with the respect they deserve. They should be. Fans pay the wages, after all – or at least they did in the days before the Sky opened. There is a varied menu at Old Trafford today, including fish and chips, pizza, chicken and hot and cold drinks. Down at the Bridge we pay more to get in and have to make the difficult culinary choice between a Wagon Wheel and a cold pasty.

In my view, Ken Bates was never very good at hiding his

disdain for traditional Chelsea fans and they for him. Ken was not going to waste good money when he didn't have to. This was the bedrock of the uneasy and uncertain relationship that was the status quo for so long. Secretly, I think Bates felt that most old Chelsea fans were thickheaded with a bent for violent and riotous behaviour and he wanted them out, but he couldn't admit publicly that they were more than the tiny minority he espoused. Also he needed them until such time in the future as they could be disposed of. They were the only people still going in his early years and their money kept the club afloat. Secretly, Chelsea fans disliked Bates too. He was not Chelsea, they suspected him of gold-digging and his abrasive personality jarred with them. But they too had to swallow: he had saved the club and he was also keeping it going. In fact he has transformed Chelsea into one of the country's top three clubs.

When Matthew Harding came along it was like a dream come true, apparently. A Shed boy who had made a few quid, wanting to buy the club. I don't think it was that simple but I could see why the masses charged to join the Harding camp. I didn't know his face until it was plastered over the papers, but that does not mean his claims of being a die-hard were untrue. Danny Baker once said a bloke approached him at Millwall and said, 'How come you didn't come down here before you were famous?'

'How do you know if I came down here or not before I was famous – you wouldn't have known my face from ten thousand others,' was Dan's entirely logical reply.

I remember one Saturday lunchtime walking into the Imperial, where Matthew was said to partake in raucous singsongs punctuated with oysters washed down with Guinness. Sure enough, over in the left-hand corner he stood, surrounded by a gaggle of middle-aged men clearly basking in his reflected glory. A tallish, elderly-looking man was looking over and smiling benevolently.

'So that's the famous Matthew Harding,' I said, nodding over as he drained his glass of Guinness. 'Looks like he's got more hangers-on than Madonna.'

'They're a good bunch,' replied the oldish man quietly.

'Do you know him then?'

'Yes, I do. He's my son.'

Meanwhile back in Manchester we hit the crossroads again where the crowd stops and the police try to keep them moving. Some are moving their legs up and down on the spot to give the appearance of mobility. City must be near and the police know it and form a line so we cannot move any further now even if we want to. More and more United are gathering behind us and applying increasing pressure on the police line. The cavalry arrive to strengthen the division between City loitering on one side and United pushing and shoving on the other.

A hail of bottles sails over our heads and smashes down among the City boys. The police immediately in front of them are scared, drawing their truncheons and lashing out at any United breaking through the other police line. They take the City fans left at the crossroads, away from the restrained United masses. A flying debris of bottles, glasses and masonry follows them. A police horse rears up, bucking and kicking, and I can see his rider has been hit. Blood is trickling from his face down on to the white collar of his shirt. The United fans cheer loudly at the first sign of claret. A policeman on foot takes the reins of the frightened horse and steadies him whilst another helps the mounted police-man from his saddle. He is obviously very shaken and sits down on the kerb looking white and disorientated, but he is soon forgotten as the hate-filled column of United fans breaks free and pursues the City contingent towards the city centre. I turn to Mike. 'If bottle throwing was an Olympic sport, one of your mob would definitely get the gold medal.'

Heading home, we stop for refreshment in a little pub just outside Northampton. Everything we had seen today we had all seen before but we were still shocked and a bit uncomfortable with the bottle-throwing finale. United didn't seem to care that among the City fans under escort were women, children and anoraks. Even the Old Bill, who eventually got hit, were only doing their job – providing protection that, frankly, I reckon United needed more than City. Seasoned football mobs should not – and most *do* not – involve innocent bystanders.

The following morning I'm sitting at the kitchen table full of the joys of spring. I've just taken the dogs out in the fresh air and Mandy has put a mouth-watering plate of eggs and bacon in front of me. The phone rings and it is Mike, barely able to contain his excitement.

'Seen the papers, Martin?'

'Not yet. Why?'

'It kicked off big time in the town centre. A City supporter lost an eye.'

I push the plate away.

FOUR

The Gooners

'There is developing a strong alternative culture to the aggressive behavioural norm that existed at football a decade ago.'

Football Supporters' Association,
The Guardian, 12 November 1990

The first time I ever set foot in Highbury was an Arsenal v. Manchester United fixture in the late '60s. Labour were in power, *Coronation Street* was the most-watched TV programme, the Bee Gees were in the charts and United were the premier soccer side. Nothing changes. I'd gone with a load of kids from around south London who were, I suppose, the early Cockney Reds. As I have recounted elsewhere, they took a large slap that day. A couple of seasons later I was back, this time with Chelsea. I can remember the Chelsea boys singing a song that went something like this:

Bertie Mee said to Bill Shankly,
Have you heard of the North Bank, Highbury?
Shanks says no, I don't think so,
But I've heard of the Chelsea Aggro.

The songs may have been amusing but the tonking we took in the visitors' Clock End was not. Arsenal had a formidable mob then. Led by Johnny Hoy (who is probably

72

knocking sixty now!) for a period in the late '60s and early
'70s, I reckon they were the top firm in the country. The
sight of Johnny and his boys running United out of the
North Bank remains with me to this day. Skinheads, braces,
Levis and Dr Martens were the order of the day, but this lot
were so smart yet so menacing. They wore creased Ben
Sherman shirts, shiny Levi sta-prest trousers and heavy black
Ivy brogue shoes that clanked loudly across the terrace
because they were all fitted with Blakey quarter-tips in the
heels and soles. Some of the older boys from around my way,
like Steve Harris, Stan Jackson and the Millet brothers,
followed the Gunners home and away and I would listen
intently to their stories of turning over rival supporters up
and down the country.

On the field Arsenal had not yet become boring. It was
easy to see why the fashion-conscious skinheads were
attracted to them. Charlie George, for one. He was their
long-haired, lanky striker and you just knew that only a
quirk of fate and a bit more footballing flair than the average
boy had stopped him exchanging blows with you on the
North Bank or in the Shed. Johnny Radford, one of his
forward partners, sported a tattoo on his arm, thus,
unintentionally, identifying himself with the terraces. And
when, for a short period, the Scottish George Best – Peter
Marinello – had the world at his feet, he elected to join the
Gunners.

A couple of seasons on and we were packed tightly in the
covered part of the Shed to shelter from the drizzle and the
wind on a cold, damp night. We were taunting the Arsenal
fans about getting wet where they stood on the open terrace
of the North Stand. We also sang, 'You'll never take the
Shed, you'll never take the Shed, e-i-adio, you'll never take
the Shed.' We had some front singing that, because Arsenal
at that time regularly showed up in our highly prized and
notorious home end and more often than not forced a timid

Chelsea crowd out without a punch or a kick being exchanged. But this night it was getting close to kick-off and they had not shown. Chelsea were beginning to think that the north Londoners had bottled. Eccles and the Webb brothers were holding court just a few steps down from where we stood. Eccles's brow was furrowed as he scanned the surrounding crowd for signs of infiltration.

I pulled up the collar of my black Harrington jacket in a vain attempt to protect me from the conditions and watched the rain hit the concrete of the dog track that encircled the pitch. The teams came out to an unusually muted reception. There is nothing worse than watching football in the pissing rain. Perhaps that's why Arsenal had not put in an appearance in the Shed. Having a fight in the pissing rain is not much fun either.

No one clapped the teams on, preferring instead to leave their hands in the warmth of their sheepskin and Crombie pockets for a minute longer. 'Arsenal, where are you? Arsenal, where are you?' sang the Shed as they twisted their clenched fists in the air. 'The wankers sign' is the universal term. Why young men choose the term 'wanker' as an insult is beyond me, wanking being the one thing they all have in common.

'The Ar-sen-al! The Ar-sen-al!' A thirtyish man of Mediterranean appearance had ducked under the crush barrier and stood facing the Shed in its entirety. 'The Ar-sen-al! The Ar-sen-al!' He snarled again, his face contorted with hate and his muscles twitching with adrenaline. He waved around a rolled-up umbrella and swivelled from side to side, beckoning anyone and everyone to take a pop at him.

'Come on, Chelsea, I'm in your fucking end!'

Far from taking a pop at him, the Chelsea Shed backed away. One solitary man. Then half a dozen skinheads joined him on either side, simultaneously unbuttoning the Crombie overcoats they were wearing like a 1970s Philadelphia soul group ritualistically unbuttoning their waistcoats on stage.

What now? Were they going to pull out hammers or knives? The coats fell open to reveal red-and-white Arsenal scarves tied around their waists.

The more senior Chelsea boys made a half-hearted attempt to repel the Arsenal invaders, but the numbers were increasing by the second. Red-and-white scarves were appearing from the insides of jackets and coats all over. Whatever was happening on the pitch was of absolutely no interest. The taking of a large home end was a spectacle to behold. Although a twenty-foot gap had opened up between the Gooners and us, they were pushing forward – knowing that the taking of the Shed was again within their grasp.

The elderly Greek gentleman with the umbrella was bashing all around him, using his brolly as a cosh. I say 'elderly' because, remember, at this time the average age of a Shed boy was about sixteen. You don't expect to be up against men in their thirties. Men almost old enough to be your dad. Mind you, it wasn't his age on my mind – I rather fancied he had something resembling lead piping inside that rolled-up umbrella. People were going down and not getting up. He reminded me of the Penguin, the comic character from *Batman* on the television. All he needed was the top hat, the cigarette holder and the Penguin laugh – wha wha wha wha.

We could have done with the Caped Crusader at this point because hundreds of Arsenal were swarming up the terrace from the sides. Where the fuck had they all come from? Surely Eccles, when doing his reconnaissance, staring across the terraces, must have realised half the faces in the Shed were unfamiliar? The reinforcements were all old too. Mind you, I hadn't even left school, so anyone over eighteen was old to me. But these blokes had strong shaving shadows or even beards. Their big hands showed the wear and tear of manual work. To a man (or a boy), Chelsea ran, and Arsenal quickly filled the vacated spaces. The Shed had fallen and it was now the turn of the north Londoners to take the piss out of the Chelsea boys standing sullenly on the fringes in the teeming rain.

A couple of seasons later Arsenal were again in the Shed but this time the Chelsea boys put up a real fight to keep hold of the end and restore some pride. Arsenal had turned up singly or in pairs, hiding their colours. Unlike now, when a mob will not be seen dead in colours, scarves or replica shirts, in those days the club's identity was worn with pride. The Gooners started to gather together on the left-hand side of the Shed. This time they were spotted and the whole Shed pushed over towards them. To everyone's surprise, Arsenal panicked and started to run. In their haste, many stumbled on the terrace steps and were left helpless as the Chelsea boys steamrollered over them in pursuit of those still beating a retreat.

About turn! The boys immediately in front of me were suddenly running back into us and I couldn't comprehend what I was seeing. They were covered in yellow paint and some were screaming. I think they had been watching too much of the Vietnam war on the news. Anyone would think Arsenal had just dive-bombed them from above and sprayed them with yellow liquid napalm. Splashes of yellow were all over, and for sure it stopped the Chelsea boys in their tracks. I swerved out of the way sharpish. No way was I risking ruining my prized tank-top jumper and Oxford bag trousers. Bemused policemen fought their way to the centre of the trouble, disarmed the Dulux infantry and put a cordon around the remaining Arsenal fans.

The Chelsea Shed interpreted these events as a great victory. They joined in the pre-match ritual of singing 'The Liquidator' by Harry J and the Allstars with euphoric enthusiasm. Greenaway and Eccles shook hands and slapped one another's backs.

'Next season, we take the North Bank,' announced Eccles.

And that is what we did. And several times after that. We'd take the North Bank and hold the Shed. The once-great Arsenal mob were in decline. Who knows why? They were an old mob then, so perhaps those guys – Penguin and company – got married or went to prison or something. Maybe they started to earn serious money on their market stalls or in their kebab shops and maybe there was no one around to step into their Gibson smooths. Chelsea were a young mob then. That's why the Arsenals, West Hams and Millwalls didn't take us too seriously in those days. Our day was to come.

But all the top mobs experience periods of strength and periods of decline. Key figures get nicked, others get married and raise families, and many just grow out of it. However, when a mob does lose a key player, that can be it. Strange, really, because there is no way that the power of any mob is dependent on one person. More often than not, the leaders are not the best fighters or the bravest in battle. There is more to it. But one season a firm can be going around the country going through anything that moves and the next, following the incarceration or retirement of one of their leaders, every tin-pot mob will be turning them over.

The pulling power of the big names was bigger than they probably ever imagined. A mate of mine, who was a big Eccles follower, told me about how one season in the late seventies when we were playing West Ham away, a meet had been arranged for midday outside the Shakes at Victoria, from where they would all travel up to Upton Park together. When he arrived there were a good couple of hundred waiting. In other parts of London, Babs and Icky would be meeting up with their boys. Time passed and Eccles had not shown. The mood of the boys changed from excited and up for it to morose and nervous. After an hour and a half it was obvious he was not coming. The mob disintegrated, walking away in groups to different pubs or furtively catching the tube in pairs. Many did not even attend the match.

I remember an incident that illustrates the other side of the coin. Years later we were up at Roker Park for an important cup game. Chelsea had taken thousands and we had filled the away end. A story was going around that Eccles, who had not been sighted at Chelsea for some seasons, was coming out of retirement for this one and he had taken a handpicked firm to Newcastle, from where they were catching the Metro to Sunderland to avoid the Old Bill. Apparently they had a batch of tickets for Sunderland seats. In the excitement, we had almost forgotten the rumour when a rumbling indicated something amiss in the seats to our right. A small group of men had arrived in the big stand and were fighting their way down to a lower tier. A grand entrance. Vintage Eccles. To this day I don't know if it was Eccles, but the crowd wanted to believe it. Even now, thirty years on from the heydays of some of these characters, you will hear people who were not born when yellow paint flew around the Shed saying knowingly 'Greenaway was there' or 'I saw Eccles marching around the town'.

Those days of umbrellas, blue Ben Shermans and yellow paint almost take on a warm hue compared to the rivalry between Chelsea and Arsenal in the early '90s, after it had taken a seriously violent turn. I think this shift in relations started when we were entertaining them at the Bridge one season. A useful contact of ours was a well-known ticket tout around the London grounds and he mentioned that a mate of his had offloaded a hundred tickets to a top Arsenal face. Before the game, the pubs were buzzing with the anticipation of the Gooners making a guest appearance in the West Stand. This part of the ground was at that time where all the old boys and the game youngsters gathered – the only bit of the ground that would have offered Arsenal any kudos should they infiltrate it.

'Bet the bastards don't turn up,' Dave sneered as we made

our way from the pub to the ground. 'Remember last year when they did turn up? Two hundred strong, they came swaggering down the Fulham Road. Saw about twenty of us outside the pub and what did they do? Crossed the fucking road!'

Dave shook his head, apparently still amazed by this unforgivable act of cowardice. I remember it well because as they passed us, bringing up the rear was my old mate Denton.

'What you doing at the back, Denton?' I asked as I walked over the road to greet him.

He stopped in his tracks, looked at me nervously and stuck his hand out.

'Fucking hell, Martin – how you doing?'

'I thought you'd be up the front, Denton,' I replied, ignoring his proffered hand.

'No, not today. I'm keeping a low profile.'

'Why bother coming, then, if you're keeping a low one?'

'I got a pull the other week so I'm on a curfew and have to sign on Saturdays at me local Old Bill shop.'

He'd put on a bit of weight since I'd last seen him, when Melvyn had chased him up the road at King's Cross. As we stood talking, his discomfort increased as his army carried on walking up the road, not knowing, or not wanting to know, that their leader had been diverted.

'Looks like your troops have deserted you,' I observed as I blocked his way. What neither of us knew was that Roy had scooted up to the Gunter Arms and alerted the firm in there that the Gooners were coming past. Denton's mob, who had been brimming with confidence only minutes before, were soon running for their lives past their leader and us, with the Gunter lot in hot pursuit. Denton did not know what to do. Did he run or did he stay chatting to us?

'You're best off staying here, I reckon,' I said, reading his thoughts. He took my advice and we stood together and watched the police intervene and drive the Chelsea fans back up the Fulham Road towards the ground. The Gooners followed but this time they walked along with heads down, even with the good police escort they now had. Denton followed a few yards behind as they were herded into the North Stand. Minutes later I stood at the top of the West Stand steps, from where I had a clear view of the North Stand entrance. I could see that the solitary figure of Denton was taking shit from a small group of up-and-coming Chelsea boys. This was like manna from heaven to these aspiring football thugs. Doing the famous Denton, even though he was alone, would be a prize to be savoured. I learned later that they missed the game, following Denton back down to Fulham Broadway tube, where they continued to give him plenty of gip until he jumped on the train and went back to the relative tranquillity of whatever north London police station he was signing on at.

Today Dave is still banging on about Arsenal's arsehole problem. 'Even if they do show, all they'll do is slap up a few scarves outside the Shed.' The rest of us are not so sure. Our friend the tout wouldn't wind us up and why buy the tickets if you don't mean to come?

'I'll have a tenner with you, Dave, that they show.'

Dave slapped my hand gypsy-style.

'That's the easiest tenner I've ever won,' I smiled.

Dave looked puzzled. He was facing the tea bar as we bantered and I was looking over his shoulder.

'Stop admiring those meat pies and pasties and turn round and look at the entrance at the bottom of the steps. Look at all them faces. Pakistanis, Turks, Greeks, Azerbaijanis and Eskimos don't follow Chelsea.'

Dave turned slowly as if not to arouse undue suspicion. 'Fuck me – they're here.'

Not a word was spoken but pies were hurriedly swallowed or discarded and drinks knocked back as we all positioned

ourselves along the walls and out of view of the entering
Arsenal mob. They only had a handful of Old Bill with
them. We waited until they were all through the turnstiles
and had moved across the short concourse and then up the
steep concrete steps that led to the back of the West Stand.
Just as our tout man had said, they were around a hundred
strong. One of their top boys was at the front. A rare white
face in this multi-cultural mob. As he reached the top stair
we stepped out of the shadows and before they could catch
their breath one of ours addressed the Arsenal paleface.
'Hello, Miller.'

We literally fell on to them, our sheer weight forcing them
back down the stairs. Those Gooners that could jumped the
turnstiles and ran back on to the Fulham Road. The others
had no choice but to try and fight us off until the police
rescued them. Which they did all too quickly. And because
they had legitimate tickets, the police insisted on leading
them in to their seats in the middle of us lot. Judging by the
number of empty seats around them, about seventy of the
original hundred had had it away over the turnstiles.
Nevertheless, they had shown, some had had a go and the
stakes had undoubtedly been raised.

The following season Chelsea negotiated a keen price for
two hundred tickets for the lower seats in the West Stand at
Highbury. The same tout who had sold the Gooners their
tickets for Stamford Bridge supplied us. We all met up at
midday on the day of the game at the York pub. By half-past
there were a good three hundred of us so we decided to head
for Highbury and take over one of their boozers. We jumped
on the Victoria line to Finsbury Park and walked out on to
the street, only to be faced by what seemed to be an almost
equal number of police coming towards us. But they simply
stood in the middle of the road, held up the traffic and
allowed us to cross. Result. They carried on up the road
without giving us a second look.

Next, we alighted on the Arsenal Tavern and walked straight in. The few Arsenal fans who were scattered around drinking couldn't believe this unexpected invasion and made themselves scarce. The guvnor went through the motions of asking a few of us who we supported but was pulling the first pint before he had an answer. The sight of scores of twenty-pound notes being waved around soon settled any unease the influx might have caused him. He had four or five staff who at his instruction jumped off their stools and away from their Saturday *Sun* and began to harvest the waiting cash.

A single policeman entered the throng, spoke to the publican, surveyed the situation and quietly left. But as sure as shit smells, he was back, ten minutes later, with fifty colleagues.

'Right, you lot!' he shouted above the din that is a furiously busy pub. 'No one drink up. Put your glasses and bottles down and make your way to the exit.'

No one took a blind bit of notice and we simply carried on chatting, drinking and puffing on fags. Some grinned at him sympathetically, like you might at a bible-basher trying to preach at you on the racecourse.

'I said, please make your way out on to the street!'

His face was getting redder and redder and his voice louder and louder but still he was universally ignored. He dragged a chair over and stood on it.

'Please can I have your attention!' he bellowed. 'I am an officer of the law and I demand you leave this pub now!'

For a minute I thought he was going to add 'in the name of Her Majesty the Queen', but his switch into *Dixon of Dock Green* speak spurred some movement as a few shuffled in the direction of the door and his officers rounded up the rest.

There was still an hour to go before kick-off and the police shoved us off in the direction of the ground. We couldn't believe it when they didn't follow. Unbelievably, they stayed put at the pub. Now, tell me who really is the mindless minority? There we were, Chelsea's main mob, drinking peaceably in a pub, but the police had turned us out, pointed us in the direction where we were more likely to clash with opposing supporters and left us to find them unescorted. We nicked a left, then a right, then another left. We really were on our own and, as luck would have it, suddenly we came face to face with another pub, this time packed with Gooners inside and out. We walked straight over to them. Most elected for safety in numbers and squeezed back inside.

As I was about to walk through the door of the pub, I noticed a geezer to my side lift a bottle above his head. Before he could crack that down on my nut or anyone else's, I hit him with an uppercut. His legs buckled and the door burst open with the Arsenal cavalry charging out to help him. But we didn't move, absorbed their initial push and then forced them back through the door. The police (a different lot) appeared and moved us on again. Shooing us off like we were suspected of stealing lemon bon-bons from a sweet shop.

A couple more turns down side streets and we found ourselves facing the main entrance of the Highbury stadium. There was a token Arsenal mob trailing us, ensuring they were safely behind the walls of police that now lined the route. Two West Ham boys were with us, Chris and Cooperman, and we were laughing about the look on the face of the Gooner I had chinned back at the pub when we ran into Black Willie and a small but familiar firm.

'Looks like you've got a fan club,' said Willie, pointing at the Arsenal hyenas on the other side of the road. A copper on a horse rode alongside us.

'Move on, gents,' he urged as he gently sidestepped his horse's arse into our faces.

'It's like kissing the old woman,' said Cooperman.

'I hope her breath smells better than that,' I replied.

As we found our entrance, the Gooners mob plucked up

courage for the row and appeared in the road immediately in front of us.

'Keep walking,' hissed Jeff. 'They won't stand.'

Bang. I'd taken a powerful smack in the side of the head. I cursed myself for not seeing him but before I could respond a copper had wrestled him to the floor. Another Gooner did stand. In front of Jeff.

'Come on, you Chelsea slag!'

Jeff kept walking but just lifted his leg higher than his normal stride and toe-punted the bloke in the nuts. Alex, my Jock mate who normally follows Celtic, loved it.

'Fuck me, Martin. Who said there was nae trouble at the fitba nae more?'

As we turned the corner opposite the Arsenal tube station, another Gooner mob thought now was a good time to attack and they came straight into us. Again I was caught from behind and this time the blow really hurt me. The brave man who had laid one on me must have been wearing a big sovereign ring because it left a hole in my upper neck and the cut was stinging like fuck. Mind you, we still tore into this lot and, ironically, they didn't run until the tube station disgorged a train full of Shed boys who dutifully chased them up the street.

Things then calmed down a bit. Jerry Kilburn spotted a few senior Arsenal faces lounging against a railing, having just been spectating at the last few minutes of rucks.

'All right, girls?' Jerry teased.

'Where the fuck have you been all day?' demanded Roy accusingly, but acknowledging that the Arsenal we'd exchanged pleasantries with so far were not their main firm.

'Shit oot as per usual,' chimed in Scottish Alex, who has now elevated himself to an authority on violence at London football derbies.

'We've been waiting in the Favourite for you lot,' explained one.

'Where the fuck is the Favourite?' I asked.

'Off the Holloway Road.'

'And we're meant to know that, are we?' I countered sarcastically.

'Let's do these tossers,' decided Alex, who didn't really understand the score. Jerry stepped in front of Alex and told the Gooners we would visit this Favourite after the game and they should make sure they didn't decide to go drinking at another obscure pub. I saw Giles in the ground and neither he nor any of his lot had heard of this pub the Favourite – if this was Arsenal's pub then it was news to all of us. No trouble in the seats either. It soon became apparent that the Gooners sit in the upper tier of this stand.

'Wait till I see that tout bastard!' fumed Dave.

After the game we hung about for their boys in the upper tier but they never materialised. The police gave us an escort of sorts back to Finsbury Park tube station, by which time they had lost interest, and about fifty of us nipped into the pub opposite for a drink. Icky and Melvyn popped in and told us that a good mob had slipped the lead and were hunting around for the Favourite and they were going to take the tube and try and join them. Me, Ally and a few others decided to do the same thing about ten minutes later. On arriving at Holloway Road, we were fucked on account of the lifts (surprise, surprise) being out of order. No one on the Holloway Road had heard of this pub and we could not find it anywhere. We were rapidly reaching the conclusion that this had been a classic wind-up. Arsenal had Chelsea hunting around north London for an imaginary pub.

Gangs of youngish black kids were watching us from across the road. When they saw us see them, they shot off.

'Spotters,' I cleverly deduced. 'What do we do now? Carry on trying to find Icky and the boys, wait for the spotters to bring back a mob, or fuck off?'

In the event, we decided to head back to Victoria and have

a drink. Ensconced in the York about an hour later, we saw some of our lot begin to drift in. Tony eventually appeared and it was obvious by his demeanour that something had gone wrong.

'Did you find them?' I asked.

'Did we find them?' repeated Tony scathingly. 'We came out at Holloway Road and had a scout round a few of the side streets but couldn't find this Favourite boozer anywhere. But we did find one called the George, which had a mob drinking outside. We thought it was you lot or something but the pub emptied and they came charging up the road at us. We let 'em use up all the bottles, glasses and ashtrays they had as ammo and then chased them back into the pub. We done the windows too and felt well pleased with ourselves. Thirty of us doing so well against a much bigger mob. But we still can't make out where everyone else is. We know you all come looking for the Favourite too.

'Anyway, back by the station we've loosened up a bit and some of us have gone in a shop for a well-earned Coke and some fags. This little mob comes around the corner but when they see us they just fuck off. I thought nothing of it, didn't even bother calling anyone out the shop. Then they came back around the corner and this time there was about fifty of them. We didn't even think about it, even though it was obvious this lot meant business. But they ran as well – but we found ourselves running into an even bigger mob. About two hundred, I reckon, and some of them tooled up. It was murder. They were picking up anything – traffic bollards, the lot – and we were getting hammered. Marcus went down and someone slashed him. I didn't see, I was getting hit from so many directions and in so many different places. I was fighting – we were all fighting – for our lives. I'm just thinking, leave us alone, you cunts. Leave us alone.

'And then, music to my ears, a sound better than an ice-cream van when you're a kid – a police siren. The Arsenal lot scatter and leave us to pick ourselves up. Marcus's clothes are hanging from his back and it looks like he's been slashed from his neck down to the cheeks of his arse. He and a couple of others somehow managed to flag down a passing cab to get to a hospital. We ran down the tube and just managed to leap on to a train as the doors shut on the Old Bill chasing us. It was just like in a film. We'd have been well nicked.'

This sounded really nasty and I could see that even Tony, a veteran of many a battle, was shaken up a bit. I realised how close we'd been to being part of it. That little bunch of spotters I had spied was, I reckon, the first lot Tony had noticed.

Soon after, I spoke to Marcus. He told me they had demanded the taxi take them to a south London hospital even though he was pissing blood. He didn't fancy bleeding to death north of the river. Marcus had over two hundred stitches put into the wound. He said he remembered being bashed over the head and going down and still being conscious as the mob clamoured to boot him in the face and body. Then he heard someone screaming maniacally, 'Out the way! Out the way! I'm gonna open the cunt up!' Marcus said it was a good job the sirens sounded then because he doesn't think whoever it was intended to stop there.

The following season, the meet for Arsenal away was at the Holloway Tavern, right next door to the station. I met Ally and a few others at Victoria and we travelled up together. At Holloway Road we took the stairs whilst Muscles and some others waited for the lift. Muscles wasn't one to have to watch the calories, weighing all of six stone.

In the sunlight, a solitary copper was waiting to greet us.

'Afternoon, Mr King, Mr McLean.'

'Hello, officer. Taking in a few rays?' I said as the sun beat down on us.

'No, I'm here to keep tabs on you lot.'

'No worries today. There'll be no trouble.'

'What about revenge for last season?'

'Don't know what you mean.'

We exchanged knowing smiles and he politely declined my offer of a drink in the pub.

Muscles and company emerged from the station mumbling something about fucking lifts not working and we all went into the boozer. Within an hour the pub was heaving, the grapevine communication of our meet working particularly well. At the end of the bar, Marcus was persuaded to take off his shirt and show the scar on his back. It was still raw and raised and his flesh looked like it had crudely been sewn back together. Which, of course, it had. The impromptu display had the effect of incensing everyone in the bar.

'Fucking cowardly bastards!'

'Let's make 'em pay!'

The mood was nasty. This was going to be no ordinary ruck. What had been done to Marcus had personalised things. It wasn't even about pride. It was about ethics.

'A few of the boys are going around to the Favourite to see if they can find out who cut Marcus. I'll see you back here in a minute,' said Ally very calmly.

'Don't be daft. If you're going, so am I.'

We followed five others out the door for the short walk to the Favourite (by now we knew it did exist and where it was). As we approached the doorway, all seven of us, the Gooners outside drank up and rushed back inside. Ally was the first in. It was like he was reading from a prepared statement.

'The cowardly tosser that cut our boy is a disgrace. If you are in here now, step outside and let's have it. One to one. No blades.'

Unlike the policeman in the Arsenal Tavern a couple of seasons back, Ally had the undivided attention of every single person. Some of them even seemed genuinely ashamed as they looked pointedly into their beer. We stood there for several crucial silent seconds. Spaced out like the Magnificent Seven. There were at least one hundred and fifty boys in there and by their own claims this was their main boozer. Yet not one word was uttered by them. No one shaped up to us. We had right on our side. They knew it and we knew it.

The police arrived outside and we stepped backwards out of the pub door. Arsenal suddenly felt brave and a few of them streamed out of the pub.

'Come on, Chelsea – let's do it!'

Going through the motions.

'Fuck off!' I dismissed them. 'You're only there with a blade in your hand or the Old Bill protecting you.'

The police went through the usual old pony of taking our names and addresses (which they knew) and warned us that if they saw us again that day we were nicked. But by now the rest of the Chelsea mob had arrived from Holloway Road and Arsenal again made another backwards dash into the Favourite. A police carrier van appeared. It drove through the Chelsea fans and stopped between the pub and us. This gave Arsenal the comfort they needed and they began to launch us with bottles and glasses from the bar. Marcus climbed on to a garden wall, crouched with his back facing the Arsenal and rolled his shirt up again.

'This is what you dirty scum did, but I'm still here!' he shouted defiantly over his shoulder whilst jabbing his finger at his back. A pint glass sailed over towards him but with the grace and sureness of an accomplished cricketer he turned and caught it effortlessly with his other hand. We all roared and clapped as Marcus returned the glass forcefully back into the Arsenal lot.

FIVE

Bursting Bubbles

'There is certainly much evidence that new fans are being recruited from the high-salary, university-educated, middle-class band. In the '80s, the game had a poor public image, but today it has a social cachet and an altogether more sophisticated, glitzy appeal that higher earners want to be associated with.'

John Williams, Leicester University,
Sunday Telegraph, 17 August 1997

West Ham means different things to different people. Football purists love them. For them, West Ham conjures up an image of a side that consistently plays attractive football at the expense, most of the time, of winning trophies. A team that provided the axis of the only England side to deliver a World Cup. A club that became known as the Academy of Football and produced such gentlemen footballers as Bobby Moore, Geoff Hurst, Martin Peters and Trevor Brooking. But for terrace purists, West Ham has always meant something very different. Something very ungentlemanly. The fans. The ICF, or InterCity Firm, as they liked to call themselves. Since the 1960s (and indeed before as, like Millwall, incidences of crowd disturbances have been recorded from way back), West Ham have had the reputation of being the country's toughest band of supporters. Millwall have always vied for the title but more people have had direct experience of West Ham due to the fact that throughout most of the last forty years they have played in the top division, whilst Millwall have played mainly in the lower divisions.

When I first visited Upton Park in the early '70s, I was shocked to see the beatings being dished out to schoolboys by men old enough to be their fathers and, in some cases, grandfathers. It was fitting that I took my first football pasting there. We did reasonably well against them that day, but not as well as the Chelsea Stockwell mob who had got in the North Bank the previous year and run the Hammers on to the pitch. I have spoken to a few veterans of that particular battle and they have told me that the truth was that the glory was short-lived. When West Ham composed themselves, they forced Chelsea into a corner and battered them for the remainder of the game. One fella I spoke to was so trauma-tised by the experience he never went to another football match. Man United were another club who took West Ham's North Bank in those days, and Johnny Hoy's Arsenal also had a pop but apparently came unstuck. Soon, unlike Arsenal, Chelsea and Spurs, who regularly took or tried to take each other's ends, no one ventured into West Ham's North Bank. As the '70s progressed, so fearsome did West Ham's reputation become that few plucked up courage to visit Upton Park at all as a mob.

The laid-back policing had something to do with it, I'm sure. There seemed to be little effort put in from the police in keeping the fans segregated. At Upton Park station, West Ham's boys would be waiting to greet you, and then, if you were fortunate enough to make it to the ground, they'd attack you as you queued at the turnstile. Inside, West Ham would normally stand next to you on a one-for-one basis in the South Bank part of the ground. I wonder if there was some visionary police strategist over in east London who was testing out some sort of 'jungle' theory about survival of the fittest, coupled with the utilisation of scarce resources. I really do believe that West Ham and the Old Bill had a special relationship. Not in a sneaky, Leicester City sort of way. Instead the police respected the boys and were, I think, quite proud of them. In a way it was a reflected glory for them. Both sides had drawn up a set of rules and for the large part they abided by them.

Leaving the ground was no easier, as you were scanned time and time again by older men looking for the merest giveaway that you were a follower of Arsenal, Tottenham, Chelsea or, God forbid, the arch-enemy Millwall.

Back in 1975, I went with West Ham to Arsenal in the quarter-finals of the FA Cup. My mate Kevin was a big Hammers fan, not really a rucker but he knew a lot of their VIPs, and somehow he had blagged a couple of tickets for the game. The match was sold out and I must admit that when I saw touts outside the ground selling tickets for four times the cover price I was sorely tempted to offload mine for a tidy profit. But I resisted, not wanting to offend Kev and because the carnival atmosphere at the game was infectious.

West Ham filled up the Clock End part of the ground as well as both sides and there was even a noisy Hammer presence in the North Bank. It is strange but sometimes this happens at games. It was like West Ham knew that they were going to win the cup and that this was part of a historic build-up to a historic victory. And Arsenal knew, too, practically vacating their ground for the visiting fans. Hostilities were therefore on hold. The sort of game Nick Hornby remembers. West Ham's anthem 'I'm Forever Blowing Bubbles' floated over the stadium as the east Londoners celebrated in advance. The media back then portrayed West Ham fans as cuddly old cockneys singing this old folk song, but as any Chelsea fan who was present in the Shed on the occasions that West Ham took it in the '70s will tell you, these lines often preceded a vicious onslaught.

It pissed down and everyone got drenched, but this did

not detract from the joy of West Ham fans as a little-known signing from lowly Rochdale, Alan Taylor, scored twice, thereby putting the Hammers one game away from Wembley. Steve Coogan's northern prat character Paul Calf looks like he was based on Alan Taylor, who, of course, went on to set Wembley alight and then slowly but surely disappeared from the limelight.

Millwall were one team who *would* turn up at Upton Park in their thousands whatever the era. I went to one of those clashes and it sticks in my mind as being the first time I saw a police helicopter being used to monitor football fans. Millwall took not one but two massive mobs that day. I was with the one that assembled at Elephant and Castle and I swear there were well over a thousand blokes milling around. The other firm had arranged to meet at Surrey Docks and the plan was to merge at Whitechapel station and then proceed to the stadium together. However, because the size of the mob at the Elephant surpassed even the most optimistic estimates, we decided to press ahead alone.

At Upton Park station we had intended to wait for the train behind, which was also full to the brim with Millwall, but the excitement and power of the crowd propelled us straight out into the street. A ticket inspector held out his hand expectantly and asked politely for our tickets. He must have been joking – we were that crammed together we could barely blink, let alone fish around in our pockets. A couple of mounted policemen tried to break up the mob a bit as we burst out of the entrance and, sure enough, a curious West Ham firm was there waiting. But Millwall were too big and too mobile for them to have any effect and they were literally carried backwards down the road whilst being punched and kicked at the same time. 'Millwall! Millwall!' we droned.

Unlike other clubs, Millwall never fuck around or waste energy singing too much. Their back-catalogue is relatively small. Outside the North Bank, a tastier West Ham mob appears and steams straight in. Two hundred one-on-one fights must be taking place. The police are panicking as they see their carefully laid plans disintegrate before them. It wasn't like this on the blackboard at their eleven o'clock briefing. They let the dogs go and this just adds to the pandemonium. Shouting, screaming, barking and sirens.

In the centre of the mêlée is an elderly man in a white coat. He wears a leather satchel draped across his shoulder and brandishes a small magazine. 'Programmes, programmes! Get yer programmes!' he shouts above the din, seemingly oblivious to the fact that World War III has broken out around him. He's got some bollocks, I think, and it crosses my mind he might be Kate Adie's dad. If not, definitely ex-military. He's got a job and he's going to do it.

We're fighting but we're moving forward and we reach the South Bank. I know from experience that there will be an even bigger show from West Ham here. There is, but it is impossible to say who, if anyone, is coming out on top. Both sets of supporters are somehow moulded into a queue for the turnstiles and the fighting continues as, one by one, battered men and youths are clicked into the ground. The man operating the turnstile I'm queuing at decides he's had enough and closes the wooden door of his 'office'. The bloke in front of me jumps and delivers a resounding flying kick to the door, and it folds up like a beach hut in a Benny Hill sketch with the attendant man beneath it. Everyone leaps the metal turnstile that is all that is left standing and charges into the ground. One young boy grabs the coins neatly set out in piles on the turnstile but sends most of them flying in his haste. A St John's Ambulance man helps the horizontal turnstile operator back to his feet.

'Fucking animals!' He waves a fist at the marauding fans. 'Fucking animals, the lot of you!'

Well, if he's going to tar me with the same brush, I'm going through too.

There is some semblance of order in the ground. The Old Bill have formed a wedge of sorts between the rival factions and are busy dipping in and pulling people out. The helicopter is up again, hovering ahead. I guess that the second train has arrived. The police are finding it hard to keep these two mobs apart. More than half the time it's easy, because the reality is that most situations like this are mass posturing and the factions don't really want to get at each other. If the police just thought 'fuck it' and walked off, I bet both sets of fans would turn around and start watching the game. Today, though, is different and the police know it. Their truncheons are drawn and they are cracking any skulls that push or fall outside of the cordons. I can honestly say that this is the only game I've been to where the trouble has persisted throughout the whole ninety minutes.

As the match ends, a voice comes over the tannoy informing the Millwall fans that they will be detained in the ground after the match for the streets to be cleared and for their own safety. Who tells them to say that? How many times have I heard it? It is a wind-up, no danger. Sure to make the detained fans all the more determined to wreak some kind of havoc. Catcalls and whistles greet the announcement and a deep-voiced fifty-year-old behind me growls back, 'We'll look after our own safety, thank you.' His cronies all laugh obligingly. So do I. He is a big fucker and I don't want him thinking I don't appreciate his sense of humour.

The police do have it sewn up outside, with more dogs on display than Crufts, and we are shoved on to a tube that does not stop at any station before Whitechapel.

I was present again, some years later, when West Ham turned the tables on Millwall. The ICF, as they were now known, turned up early for a league game at the Den. Millwall were well caught out because they had already gone looking for West Ham at Surrey Docks, only for the ICF to arrive at

New Cross Gate with no police escort and no Millwall reception committee. They spread out across the road and started to check in the pubs along the Old Kent Road. All they were going to find was us. Twenty Chelsea who had come along to align ourselves with Millwall but had decided to stay having a drink whilst Millwall toured around London playing hunt a Hammer.

We were standing outside the pub with one solitary copper whose role was pretty unclear. We stood still as five hundred of West Ham's finest strolled towards us. Natalie was at the front of the ICF and he looked over in our direction and just laughed, shrugged his shoulders and kept walking. He had been over Chelsea a few times drinking with Babs, so he knew who we were. Me, Black Willie, Roy, Manny and the rest of us couldn't believe our luck, all agreeing that it had been a close shave. The next pub down wasn't afforded the same treatment and we watched as they put the windows in and chased a handful of terrified Millwall down the road. Millwall proper started arriving back at the pub and we explained what had happened. One Millwall fella was so incensed that West Ham had been able to turn up on their manor and parade openly that he had tears of anger leaking from his eyes. 'We'll never hear the last of this,' he croaked.

They left the pub to catch up with the ICF party but knew that by now the police would be up with them. The real chance had gone and the reputational damage had been done. Some east London stragglers, obviously overconfident, got waylaid and paid a heavy price, but Millwall were standing around wagging fingers at each other and holding an inquest as to how they could have got it so wrong. If they had been a public limited company, someone would have to have fallen on his sword over such a fuck up.

Someone said West Ham were plotted up outside the Cold Blow Lane. It reminded me of the London Marathon, as everyone set off at quick walking pace and then broke into a trot. Ahead of me all I could see were hundreds and hundreds of bobbing heads. But at the CBL end we ran into a wall of police.

'West Ham on the Old Kent Road!' shouted someone.

'Fuck the Old Kent Road,' I remarked to Roy. 'If I want to take up athletics, I'll join the London Harriers. Let's go in the ground.'

We made our way to the halfway line part of the ground. West Ham had been allocated the end to our right. It was fairly empty, so we assumed the fun and games outside were still very much in progress. By three o'clock, though, everyone was in and Millwall fans clambered on to the wire fence and made furious wankers signs at the visitors. I said earlier that I have never understood why football fans think that calling each other a wanker is an insult. I can also never see the point in directing insults at a crowd of two thousand people. Who in particular are they aiming the sign at? Do they really think it upsets anyone?

Outside after the game it is dark, as it always is when you leave the Den, and we all stick together and follow Millwall's main mob down the forbidding south London backstreets that surround the ground. When we get out on to the Old Kent Road, men are streaming past us. Not panicking, but certainly running. I hear the command 'Stand, Millwall, stand', which is a dead giveaway that a mob is, or is about to be, in retreat.

'For fuck's sake, Millwall, stand!' screams one young warrior, about forty-five years old, next to us, but even he soon shows us a clean pair of heels. We duck out of the mob, stand in a shop doorway and turn into neutral observers.

'It's the ICF,' whispers Roy.

As they stream past us, we can see why Millwall's bottle has gone. This is the cream of West Ham and they mean business. They are walking quickly and confidently, in time like an army, and they are fit and in their prime. There are further confrontations in and around the various stations but, more or less indifferent in our loyalty, we were unanimously of the opinion that West Ham had taken all the honours and that on that showing there wasn't a firm to touch them. Remember, this was Millwall at Millwall.

About a year after that game a documentary was shown on national television which showed the work of a police unit working on the London Underground network. Part of the programme featured a couple of plain-clothes officers following West Ham around London, from their meet in east London to their early arrival at New Cross Gate. You could see from the film how concerned they were over the lack of police presence when West Ham appeared out of the station. They could be heard trying to alert other police on their radios. But the most telling comment of all, which perhaps underlines the fact that there is little difference between working-class policemen and working-class football hooligans, came from one officer who babbled excitedly something like, 'I don't believe it, West Ham are taking liberties – this is Millwall's manor!'

Elsewhere in the film the camera alights on us, minding our own business as we stood outside the pub watching the antics of the ICF. One copper says, 'That lot are some of Millwall's boys,' and then the camera goes on to record for posterity the West Ham smashing up the next pub along. The night of the broadcast, my telephone was red hot. 'Film star', 'Poser' and 'Millwall traitor' were just a few of the names shouted down the line at me. But, sadly, no offers of further TV work followed.

A story which earned the West Ham firm further extensive TV and newspaper coverage was when they had a famous tear-up with Manchester United on a cross-channel ferry. Both clubs were playing pre-season friendlies in Holland and that is how a couple of hundred United fans and a dozen ICF ended up on the same ferry leaving Harwich. Because of the huge difference in numbers, the two sets of fans had barely given each other a second look. The ICF settled down in one of the bars, whilst United commandeered more or less every other space on the ship.

One West Ham guy joined a group of Manchester lads who had kicked off a card school. The Londoner started to win most of the hands and because the stake money was mere pennies suggested they upped the ante. The kitty swelled but the United lot were now taking serious money off the ICF chap and he started to get the right hump. History does not tell whether the Mancs were cheating or not, but the ICF man accused them of it, threw his drink over one of his opponents and kicked the table into the air. The remaining eleven West Ham flew off their bar stools and tore into the card school but were forced back into a corner when Manchester fans from other parts of the bar and the boat joined in the battle. The Londoners were heavily outnumbered but used cutlery and crockery from the bar and kitchens to hold their own. Non-aligned members of the public dived for cover and ferry security arrived, only to realise it was a situation beyond their control. They retired to the flanks, joining the public in watching a battle that now included the wielding of fire-axes and the spraying of fire-hoses. The captain, sensibly, turned the boat around and took its warring passengers straight back into Harwich.

News had spread of a major nautical incident and back at the port police and dogs streamed on to the boat, nicking anyone who remotely resembled a football fan. Among those arrested was a fifty-five-year-old follower of West Ham. Never courtiers of publicity, the Hammers did not respond to the waiting TV and press crews, but the battered and upset Mancs did. They complained about how West Ham started it and how they were picked on. It speaks volumes for the type of firm West Ham had that a dozen could hold out for so long against a couple of hundred Manchester boys – and the Manchester boys whined about West Ham picking on them!

West Ham must be the most televised mob in history. I remember another time when a film crew followed the ICF up to Old Trafford for their annual set-to with Manchester United. The mob is seen alighting at Manchester Piccadilly, chasing off the first welcoming committee and then proceeding towards the stadium, attacking various pubs *en route*. The film records some well-known ICF faces holding an inquiry (à la Millwall) as to why some of their number were not keen to mix it with the bigger Manchester mob.

'A couple of years ago we would have gone through this lot in five seconds,' pleads one, dismissing United's firm as one would a Villa or a Southampton. United wait patiently across the road for the next round of fisticuffs as West Ham manage to rally themselves. More fighting. More arrests – but the ICF have reached the ground. Further fighting is committed to film inside the ground, and then the camera follows the ICF leaving early in order to encounter United in the Manchester backstreets. Sure enough they do, because an up-for-it Manchester firm have had the same idea. The film shows that West Ham are forced to back off from United as one solitary mounted policeman tries to quell the disturbance. I think it was just bad luck that on the day the east Londoners chose to take their very own Dr Johnson with them, they did not perform to the best of their ability.

They had it all. The numbers, the names, the bottle and the organisation. Especially the organisation. They had just the one mob (unlike some other clubs, notably Chelsea), they were highly disciplined under pressure and they organised their campaigns with military precision. They should have rented themselves to Third World countries to give advice on coups and quelling rebellions. For sure they would have fucked Saddam Hussein out of Kuwait whilst the British and Americans were still holding press conferences announcing they had decided to call the campaign 'Operation Desert Storm' or some such shit.

It is often said that the ICF are the only football firm who were able to transport their 'skills' and apply them elsewhere. When the ecstasy and rave boom swept the country in the late 1980s and early 1990s, former ICF personnel were instrumental in organising, profiting from and policing these events. Since then they have diversified into more mainstream business activities. I don't discount the possibility of ICF plc floating on the Stock Exchange some time in the future, complete with news clips of hundreds of east Londoners queuing up outside selected banks in Whitechapel to hand in their applications for shares.

That same film even showed West Ham turning up at Chelsea for a night game when they weren't even playing at the Bridge. We were hosting Sunderland in the semi-finals of the Milk Cup and West Ham were down the end of the District Line for a pedestrian league game at Wimbledon. We'd heard that the ICF were threatening to turn up for a fight on their way to Plough Lane but we dismissed this as bullshit. But, true to their word, fifty of them got off at Fulham Broadway and walked up the road towards the ground spanking anyone getting in the way who vaguely resembled a Chelsea boy. The man with the camera ran alongside. About twenty of us were standing chatting outside the North Stand gates when suddenly this West Ham firm were right on top of us.

'Come on, Chelsea,' said the weasel-faced Hammer whom I'd last clocked disappearing up the M1 with a mob of Chelsea in pursuit. Straight away someone folded a can of Tennent's into his face. Chelsea around us woke up to what was going on and a full-scale fight broke out which went up and back down the street as first one mob had the initiative and then the other. As the rowing reached the corner of Harwood Road and Fulham Road, two coachloads of Sunderland fans were disembarking from their weary journey. They couldn't believe their eyes as the police assigned to escort them to the ground left them standing at the Lord Palmerston pub whilst they intervened in the row between the two London firms. And there on the edges, jumping around in order to get the best shots, was the resident cameraman.

West Ham departed for their Wimbledon tie but Chelsea smarted over this latest liberty taken in the name of the ICF. After the Sunderland game finished, a good army of Chelsea made their way quietly down to Parsons Green and lay in wait for West Ham returning from Wimbledon on the tube. They let the first couple of trains through because only a limited number of boys were on board. But then a train packed to the rafters with ICF pulled in and Chelsea, who were five deep on the platform, mullered an unsuspecting and enclosed eastbound train full of West Ham's young lot.

Over the years, with most London derbies, things evened themselves out in the rucking stakes. One year Chelsea might do Tottenham but the following year Spurs would have the upper hand and so on. But with West Ham, even the most ardent Chelsea boy would have to admit that, although Chelsea won the occasional battle, West Ham would win the war.

That was until the early '90s, when the tide, for the first time in my experience, turned in Chelsea's favour. The ambushing of the train was seen by many as a turning point but West Ham always denied that it was their main boys on board, and even if it was, all it did was settle up the earlier fun and games around Stamford Bridge. The turning point was Parsons Green. But a different day, a different ruck.

Chelsea were entertaining West Ham on the same day as

the Oxford v. Cambridge boat race, so a good proportion of Old Bill were policing the Thames because you can never tell what those university types will get up to. We were all meeting in the Peterborough Arms on Parsons Green and my pal had told me that West Ham were also planning on drinking on the green. It is only a small place with a few pubs facing what was probably once a village green, so it was inevitable that we would find one another. We were plotted up by midday but there was no sign of West Ham. Half one and still no show. Half two and it looks like they're not coming. Not this late. I was a bit worried too that some of us had drunk a bit too much for a ruck and I remember it crossing my mind that West Ham could well have figured this. Everyone was getting restless and some suggested we went looking for them.

'If they do turn up we're going to get murdered. There's not enough of us.' This from some jerk I'd never seen before who was a ringer for Clark Kent in his horn-rimmed spectacles. We all turned and snapped at him.

'If you don't feel safe, best fuck off,' growled Mark with typical understatement.

'Point taken, chaps,' replied Superman, who had taken off his glasses, not in preparation for a row but to wipe off the saliva which had peppered his lenses when we were all spitting with anger at his remarks. You can think these things but never, ever say them. Not at a time like this.

Before abandoning the day, I decide to stroll across the green and check out the other pubs one last time. The first door I poke my head around shows the bar packed with the usual Chelsea yuppie lunchtime set. Lots of Ruperts and Camillas look over at me, a faint sign of distaste flickering across their faces as they swig from their bottles of Grolsch. There is more than a faint flicker of distaste on my face as I stare at them, all replica rugby shirts and Saab convertibles. Camilla will be inviting Rupert back to the townhouse later for a bit of horsey sex because Mummy and Daddy are up at the cottage in Norfolk.

Sitting at the bar slightly apart from the yups is a bloke I recognise from the telly. He's got a beer and a chaser and he's even wearing a fucking cravat. As I walk across the green to the next pub, I pull from the recesses of my mind who he was. He used to be in the *Doctor in the House* programmes on TV. Resting, I expect.

The next pub showed definite signs of life, and as I peered in through the window, sure enough, West Ham were in there. As I entered and walked to the bar, sixty of them looked over. As I sipped my drink, I looked over my pint glass to see if my two West Ham mates were around. It's West Ham's older lot, all right. This motley crew have been going as long as me and in a minute someone's going to fall in.

'All right, Martin?'

I looked around, and standing behind me was a West Ham fan from Mitcham I knew. In fact, we went to school together.

'Seen Mark or Barry?' I asked, referring to my two Hammer pals.

'I ain't seen them – or you, come to that – since I bumped into you all down Brighton coming out that little Indian restaurant.'

I laughed at that because it jogged my memory. I was working at Gatwick (or GatNICK) Airport and a few West Ham fans there decided to go down to Brighton to watch their team play. I tagged along with my mate Glen, the gastronomic Chelsea fan. We had a bellyful before the game and afterwards toured the backstreets and lanes of Brighton in search of an Indian restaurant, as the booze and the sea air had left us all Hank Marvin. Eventually we stumbled on a small Indian only because one of us had nipped up an alley for a piss and had smelt the unmistakable aroma of Indian food over the general odour of back-alley cat's piss, festering black bin-liners and dog shit.

Fordy had come into the possession of a credit card, so the meal was on him. 'Have what you like; this is on . . . Andrew Glover,' he announced, reading the name off the blue American Express card. We pushed two tables together, ordered twelve pints of lager for starters and took our seats. The flock wallpaper and the threadbare carpet were dead giveaways that the establishment had not been decorated since this particular family had dropped off the bottom of a juggernaut in the mid 1970s. The tablecloths were a wonderful mosaic of soy sauce, curry and vomit stains. I'd like to see Danny Baker or Shane Ritchie try the doorstep challenge here. A neon light in the window boasted that the restaurant was fully air-conditioned. All curry houses like to tell the public this, but I'm not sure why. In Bombay, an air-conditioned eating place is an asset, I'm sure, but in Britain, where, if you're lucky, a cooling system might be required for five days of the year top whack, it is a bit of an irrelevance. But there you go – no one's told them yet, twenty years on.

'Twenty popadoms, Abdul,' shouted Fordy. 'Ten plain and ten spicy,' he added, calling on his CSE in Maths.

The pressure was getting to the solitary waiter, who put down a half-pulled glass of lager, walked to the other end of the room, opened a door that led to a staircase and shouted, 'Chuda muda coulda mulla hulla chuda salah salas,' which my tourist guide to Urdu and Hindi informed me translated into something like, 'Get your arse down here, Granddad! We have that rare occurrence, an influx of customers!'

An elderly man shuffled down the stairs, pausing at the bottom to rub his eyes and survey the situation. He obediently began to ferry the Carlsberg over to our tables. He was dressed in a striped pyjama jacket with a black tank-top jumper hanging over the top. His dark jogging bottoms revealed his pyjama trousers underneath as they rode up the leg and on his head he wore a grey Cossack-style hat. It was evident that before his sleep he had been giving his grey whiskers a trim, as hairs from his beard hung in clusters all over his tank top. We couldn't stop laughing at him, although we were all loath to make it too obvious, as we knew, if we offended him too much, exactly where he would shake those hairs off.

Glen, unbelievably, hadn't had too much experience of Indian food and just repeated what he thought was Fordy's order.

'I'll have a creama koran, chicken woggle eye and bung yung bargo.'

'Pardon?' said grey beard.

'Same as Mick,' replied Glen, pointing at Fordy.

As soon as the waiter was out of earshot, Fordy turned on Glen.

'That was fucking clever, wasn't it?'

'What?'

'Calling me Mick, that's what. My name is Andrew Glover, not Mickey Ford.'

'Is it?' queried a befuddled Glen.

'Yes! Andrew Glover is the name on the card, dickhead.'

Glen fell in. 'Sorry, Mick – I mean Andrew.'

We finished the meal, which, as was to be expected, was pretty rotten. Cheap Indian meals are like rough women. You fancy them for a clearout after a night on the piss but once you've partaken you wish you hadn't. The musty and damp smell was now making me feel quite sick, but first I had to visit the toilet. This really was a shit hole, quite literally. The bowl was caked with ten years' accumulation of turds that had dodged the flushing. Smatterings of grey hair clippings told me that Granddad had used the facility recently. I was glad I only needed a piss in this cross between a poodle parlour and a latrine pit. This is another feature of high-street restaurants – and many pubs, for that matter:

they can be done up to the nines in the eating part or the bar, but the toilets are unfit for animals. You can bet your life that the lock is broken on the trap door, there is no paper and the floor is swimming in urine. Shit at your peril, dear customer. Certainly no Charlie-snorting here.

As I left the gaff, Fordy was cheerily bidding farewell to our hosts.

'See ya, Abdul!'

'See ya, Fifi!' I added, and the old man looked at us with a humble smile, clearly thinking 'English scum'. It was an exchange that summed up the relationship between the Indian restaurateur and the young English male. Mutual contempt just about held in check because they need our money and we need their curries.

Fordy came a cropper not long after when he went to a home game at Upton Park still carrying poor old Mr Glover's plastic. He walked into the club shop and loaded up on a shirt for him, a kit for his boy, a ski hat for his old woman and air freshener and stickers for the car.

'How would you like to pay?' asked the lady behind the counter.

'American Express?'

'That'll do nicely.'

Fuck me, thought Fordy, this is brand new, just like the adverts. Unlike the Pakis down in Brighton, who were still using the old-fashioned swipe system, the club shop at West Ham owned a computerised credit-card checking system.

'I'm sorry, sir, but there seems to be a problem with your card.'

Fordy had a shrewd idea what the problem was, so he grabbed the gear and sprinted out of the shop. The lady from behind the counter pursued him. He managed to lose her but her cries of 'Stop, thief!' alerted a nearby police-dog handler, who let his charge loose. The alsatian bit into Mickey's calf muscles and brought him down, then the copper jumped on top and slammed the cuffs on him. He still bears the teeth marks to this day.

Petty thieving and the raiding of shops was a very '70s and '80s thing more often than not carried out by northern supporters. Chelsea boys who got up to tricks normally did it in a bit more style. During one of Chelsea's recent European runs, all the old boys had booked into the Sheraton for a luxurious stay in one of Europe's finest cities. One well-known, semi-retired top boy was booking in at reception alongside a very famous TV pundit and former top footballer. He clocked the guy leaving his credit card behind the jump for the duration. That evening Chelsea won and it was all back to the hotel bar, where the Chelsea chap ordered champagne all round and gave the room number and name of the TV personality. 'My Diners' Club card is with reception,' he said. They ran up a bill of over a grand on the poor chap's card. No matter – he was an ex-West Ham player anyway.

Fast forward to Parsons Green, and I try to leave the pub but two men fighting a lone man on the footpath block my way. I recognise the lone man, not as a cowboy with a black mask and white Stetson but as a Chelsea fan. The two West Ham fans retreat back into the pub and the Chelsea boy follows. I hurry over to the pub where we are gathered. Looking over my shoulder, I can see that the Chelsea boy is still giving it to the east Londoners although they have spilled out on to the green and have surrounded him. He is walking backwards towards us, drawing them out whilst questioning the integrity of their mothers. Our pub door bursts open and Chelsea fly across the green towards West Ham.

'ICF, ICF!' they cry. A distress flare bangs into the air, followed by a cheer, and then another firework bangs into life. I see the red smoke fly through the space between the two mobs and the firework strikes a West Ham fan on the upper arm. Then the two sets of fans are into one another as the red mist hangs in the air. A Hammer hits the floor and this time there is no retreat as Chelsea swarm over him. Two more bangs follow in quick succession and West Ham don't like the way this has started. They are disorientated and lose their famous composure and organisation. They run in every direction, but many are felled as they flee and are dealt with seriously. Parsons Green has become a battleground, complete with smoke and prostrate bodies.

It is one of those fights where everyone has a turn. The smoke from the flares has made it difficult to distinguish who is who but it is indisputable that Chelsea are coming out in front, despite some rallying and counterattacks from West Ham. As with all football rucks, it is not long before the police arrive, driving their meatwagons on to the green in the middle of the fighting. As the doors slide open, I step back into the pub. Well, I'm almost pushed in, as a bloke behind me has the same idea. I hold the door to let him in.

'Thanks, mate.'

I look at him now, recognise the face and block his path.

'What's the matter, pal, lost yer bottle? Why don't you have it away with the rest of them?'

'I don't know what you're on about, mate. I don't even follow football.'

'Is that right? Then why have you been going to West Ham for the past twenty-five years? Go on, fuck off, you mug!' I say, staring into his eyes.

He shrugs his shoulders and walks back out into the aftermath of the battle, where the police are making themselves well busy.

This was a crushing victory against the biggest liberty-taking mob ever to visit the Bridge. In all my years I'd never seen West Ham turned over so easily and so surely as they were on this occasion. If you talk to any member of the West

Ham firm, they'll deny they were battered that day, or say that it wasn't their main mob, or that they were hit whilst they were waiting for the real faces to arrive and so on. But my pal Joe was travelling home by train later that evening and happened to share a carriage with some big West Ham faces. They didn't know him and they held a stewards' there and then. Bags of finger-pointing, blaming and accusing each other of being too old. ICF, RIP.

SIX

Nobody Liked Them

*'Ugly battles between Manchester City and Millwall fans
this weekend were pre-planned and are just the tip of an
iceberg that could destroy the game's new family image . . .
their ringleaders, nearer middle age than teenage, booked
into a plush Stockport hotel to enjoy a Saturday night out
after the day's mayhem . . . the organisers looked so
respectable, with designer gear on and Burberry jackets.
You'd think they were businessmen on a trip. I saw one of
them in the thick of it during the match and he'd been
sitting in first class reading* The Times.*'*

Eye-witness account, *Daily Mail*, 8 February 1999

'Mart! Mart!' Mandy's voice resounds up the stairs. 'Hang
on,' I hear her say. 'I think he's in the bath.' I am. She pokes
her head around the door and tells me Dave wants me on
the phone. Well, Dave will have to want. What is it about
the telephone that makes us never consider not answering it
and when we do it's compulsory that we stop what we are
doing and go to the phone. Whoever it is. Whatever we are
doing.

'Tell him I'm having a soak and I'll bell him back in a
minute.'

She does, and I slip down the enamel a bit further. The
phone goes again.

'Hello, Roy, he's in the bath. Can he call you back?'

Mandy shouts up the stairs to tell me to call Roy too. I hear her pottering in the kitchen, then the phone goes again.

'Yes, he is still in the fucking bath! You only rang a minute ago!'

Must be Dave again. Mandy's losing her rag, so I lift myself out of the bath and trot downstairs in my towel. Dave is like a kid with a new toy.

'Have you heard? We've drawn Millwall in the cup!' he bubbles. Interesting, yes – but it could have waited.

No sooner had I got rid of Dave, Roy calls back.

'I know – we've got Millwall in the cup.'

'Are you going?' enthuses Roy.

'I dunno. I've just got out the bath and getting dry is top of my list at the moment.'

'Sorry to have bothered you . . .'

I picture Roy holding the phone in front of him and staring at it confusedly, like they do on the telly. What's up with Kingy? Why ain't he excited?

And now there is someone at the fucking door. Steve, my Chelsea mate from down the road, is standing there. He ignores my state of undress.

'Have you heard?'

'Yes.'

'Are you going?'

'Yes.'

'Catch you later!'

At that he turns and heads up the garden path.

'Who is it?' shouts Mandy from the kitchen.

'It's the vicar, Mand, wants to know whether we got any old clothes or bric-a-brac for the church jumble,' I call back. 'Go on – fuck off, you ponce,' I shout at the fresh air in front of me. 'Coming round here on the earhole when I'm having me bath. Now piss off!'

As I slam the door and put on my cross face, Mandy steams out the kitchen and throws the front door open, only to see nothing. I take the stairs two at a time, laughing as she curses me. I stop laughing, though, when I heave myself back into the bath and the water's freezing cold.

The FA Cup draw was less than ten minutes old and already the Chelsea/Millwall fixture was sending a buzz around the country. I'd never been to the New sanitised Den but had enjoyed many excursions to the old, sinister one, and not only with Chelsea. I had seen West Ham, Leeds, Portsmouth, Cardiff, Birmingham, Man U and Spurs all get the Millwall welcome at various times. Die-hard Millwall fans I knew told me they didn't reckon the new ground. They said it didn't have the same intimidatory atmosphere that had hung over Cold Blow Lane. The New Den was all-seater, for one. Not conducive to creeping up on and attacking away supporters, or getting together in groups and really getting behind the team.

Because, say what you will about Millwall, here is a set of supporters who really get behind their team. I only wish they were more hospitable to visiting Chelsea fans. Considering the club has enjoyed relatively little success, the supporters are a persistent and passionate lot. Many like a row; most have a dry and very south-east-London sense of humour. Down at the Den everyone was fair game, and because of the close proximity of the crowd to the players, those who were on the receiving end of the piss-take really knew it. If a player was bald, ginger, fat, thin, tall, short or, worst of all, ex-West Ham, he'd receive an ear-bashing for ninety non-stop minutes down there. They didn't go in for clever topical songs, like at Chelsea; they preferred pure, hate-barbed, personal abuse. I stood next to a geezer down there once. He was fifty if he was a day and as the game progressed he was becoming increasingly vexed with the referee. He had the deepest, loudest voice I have ever heard – he made Greenaway sound like that comedian Pasquale – and roared insult after insult at the ref. At one point he actually said, 'Ref, I'm coming on that fucking pitch and I'm going to stick my arm up your arse and rip your fucking uterus out, I am!' No one batted an eyelid. The regulars knew him. God knows what the ref thought.

Like Chelsea, Millwall were labelled as being particularly racist, but, like Chelsea, I think this was media-driven. Millwall had a famous leader in the '70s named Tiny who was black, and as I found out from first-hand experience, they had black geezers in their mob who did the business for them. So it doesn't add up. I can testify that they treated their black players and their white players just the same. If a black player played badly, he would get stick and would get called a black bastard, just the same as if an overweight player had a bad one, they'd call him a fat bastard. Millwall were playing two black players – Phil Walker and Trevor Lee – in the mid-'70s when there were still not many black footballers in the league at all.

Contrary to popular opinion, I always found racism was far more prevalent up north. I remember going to Middlesbrough, or it could have been Sunderland, in the early '70s and a well-known and well-respected half-caste was at the front of our mob. We were all taken aback when their fans started singing to the tune of 'Que Será Será':

He's a coon, a coon
It's plain to see, to see
He's blacker than you and me
He's a coon, a coon

as if they'd never come across a black man before.

The word on the street was that we were meeting for today's cup game at a pub near Lambeth North tube station. Dave, Manchester Mike and I arrived at the Hercules at noon to find it already packed to the rafters. A man-giant was blocking my path. Now I've seen some big geezers in my time but this bloke was unreal. I'm not exaggerating when I say his arse was resting on my shoulder as I tried to pass him.

'Excuse me, mate.'

Gulliver glanced down at me blankly and moved slightly sideways. He made Dave appear thin. I didn't know him from Adam and, judging by his dismissive sneer, he didn't know me. Jerry Kilburn saw us and tugged me past him with his outstretched hand.

'He's a fucking lump,' I commented.

'Yeah, he's come up with the Bracknell lads. Apparently he doesn't even like football,' remarked Jerry.

'What with his shaved head and menacing glare, I think we can find a place for him at the front of our mob, don't you?'

Jerry chuckled. On looking around I found myself nodding like a dog on the dashboard of a Mark II Cortina. There were people in here I hadn't seen for twenty years; some I knew were at Cold Blow Lane when we got a hiding all those years ago. Hair had gone and paunches had appeared. Shoulders had collapsed a little too, and I noted the men had abandoned the shoulders-back-chest-out walk that comes with the cockiness and general feeling of invincibility that accompanies the late teens and early twenties. Some had blotchy red faces which told me they hadn't eased up on the drink, but it warmed the heart to see them. They had given up going to Chelsea many moons ago, but a match like this and they knew they were needed, so the wife had to shop on her own today, or the crib match down the working-man's club was given a miss. For one day only, these veterans were turning the clock back.

Everyone was catching up with one another. Some were amazed that me and a few of the others were still going regularly. This got me pondering. It occurred to me that most of us in here were closer to the end of our lives than we were to the beginning. Twenty years ago we were drinking, scrapping and bantering like today, yet it seemed like only last year. In twenty years' time we would be in our sixties. All bus passes and prostate problems.

'Are you still at it, then?' asked one of the old Hounslow lot.

'Now and then,' I replied, for the first time a bit embarrassed.

'I don't believe it,' said Hounslow, shaking his head. 'I have trouble getting in and out of the car these days.'

The pub was becoming fuller and fuller and new arrivals were forced to stand out in the street. Whoever had picked the Hercules had it sussed – it was wedge-shaped and there was a good view of the surrounding roads and the tube station opposite. No way could Millwall bushwhack us here. I would say there were about three hundred here, and there were still two hours to go before kick-off. As per usual, though, people started to get restless and the lager prompted a good deal of fighting talk. It makes me mad because over the years that has been Chelsea's downfall. We are incapable of sticking together in one big mob. Some want to go here, some want to go there, some are meeting mates at the Elephant, some want to leave now, some want to leave later. Fucking shambles. What's that saying about too many chiefs? Well, Chelsea certainly has its fair share of chiefs, and some of them wouldn't even qualify as squaws, let alone Indians, in some other firms. Eccles once commented that lager was the downfall of the '60s and '70s Chelsea mob and Tony, years later, said the same thing applied to Charlie in the '80s and '90s.

Dave suggested we shoot off and go and meet up with Puncho, our Millwall mate, and his lot.

'You're joking, I hope,' I said, looking at him in amazement that he should consider such a thing.

'He's your mate, ain't he?'

'Yes, but I ain't going in a pub full of Millwall's nutcases today. Get real, you plank.'

Dave then suggested we jump in his motor and drive to the ground to get some tickets and have a look at what Millwall are up to. Rumour had it they were mobbing up in a pub on the Jamaica Road.

As we left, the phone rang behind the bar and an Irish barman picked it up. When he had finished the brief conversation, I heard another barman ask who had called.

'Kennington Old Bill. Wanted to know if there was a Chelsea firm in here.'

'What did you say?'

'"No." I'm not to know who these gentleman are, am I?' He laughed, motioning at the three hundred geezers surrounding him.

Not very far down the Jamaica Road, we discovered Millwall were in the said pub. If they decided to walk towards the Hercules and Chelsea towards Jamaica Road, they'd be on top of each other within fifteen minutes. We parked the car up and strolled back to the pub to have a butcher's in the windows. Manchester Mike put his hand over his brow like a seaman looking for land and said, 'Not a very good turnout for them.' He couldn't have been more obvious if he had tried.

'Shut up, for fuck's sake,' urged Dave. 'If someone hears you, we'll get slaughtered.'

We were now very much behind enemy lines. I remember watching the old black-and-white war films when I was a kid and thinking how exciting it must be to get parachuted in behind enemy lines with a nice flying jacket on. Well, we hadn't parachuted, we'd arrived in Dave's Datsun, but the feeling must have been the same.

Outside the pub, a fella was talking into his mobile phone, so we slowed down to catch what he was saying.

'Yeah . . . yeah . . . no word from the scouts . . . let me know as . . . yeah . . . yeah.'

I stopped, knelt and undid and then did up my shoelace. This was a cunning trick I had picked up from Ilya Kuryakin, the blond English one out of TV's *Man from Uncle.*

'Let's go in,' suggested Mike.

'Bollocks,' returned Dave. 'Let's *not* go in there. Let's walk around the block and jump in the car and fuck off out of here.'

Around the corner, a man standing in a shop doorway followed our progress intently. He took a mobile from his jacket pocket and began prodding furiously with his forefinger.

'We've been tumbled,' Dave observed.

Back in the safety of the car, we'd only driven a couple of hundred yards when we noticed two kids on mountain bikes leaning up against the traffic lights. One held a mobile phone. They looked like they should have been clutching Action Men, not Vodafones.

'Must be his brother's,' remarked Mike.

'Knowing the average age of this firm, it's probably his granddad's,' I laughed.

Back at the Hercules, the numbers had almost doubled since we had left and the whole surrounding area was teeming with Chelsea. A couple of blokes turned up waving tickets they had just bought down at the ground from Tweedy, a Chelsea ticket tout. Apparently he still had a good deal more to knock out. Mark raised his voice above the din and informed all and sundry that we'd be on the move in five minutes. Six hundred men nodded, agreeing like they were schoolchildren who had just been addressed by their teacher on a day visit to the British Museum. Mark turned to us and quizzed us about our sojourn into Millwall territory. How many? Old Bill with them? He was almost foaming at the mouth.

'London Bridge!' he shouted. 'Everybody catch a train to London Bridge and we'll get off there.'

The traffic came to a standstill as this huge mob crossed the road and queued in an orderly fashion to enter the station. No singing. No shouting. People just chatting quietly amongst themselves. Passing motorists could have been forgiven for thinking that this throng was just a bunch of young Christians off to see the Billy Graham Roadshow at Wembley. No hint whatsoever that this was a top soccer mob who within half an hour would be rucking toe to toe with an equally hard and willing south London firm.

Looking at the queue, we decided to drive back down to the ground, collar Tweedy for some tickets, then meet the others as they came marching down Jamaica Road. *En route* I spotted Pat, editor of *Thug Monthly*, standing on a street corner near the Millwall pub.

'Millwall are leaving the pub and coming up to meet Chelsea as they come down the Old Kent Road,' he informed me.

'But Chelsea are going nowhere near the Old Kent Road. They're getting off at London Bridge and should be strolling down here in the next ten minutes.'

'Oh, I was told they were getting out at Borough and coming through the back-doubles and on to the Old Kent Road.'

'Things have moved on, Pat.'

We had driven on a bit further when Dave spoke almost without opening his mouth. 'Don't look round but we've got the law up our arses.'

'Old Bill? Where?' asked Mike.

Dave did his Ray Alan impression again. 'Don't look now. They're right behind.'

Mike, like Ray Alan's dummy, swivelled his head around almost ninety degrees and beamed at the three officers in the carrier behind. 'So they are.'

They sounded the siren and flashed the blue light, giving us the impression they wanted us to pull over. The young copper sitting next to the driver got out and walked to Dave's door.

'Would you mind getting out of the car please, sir?'

His courteous manner made me think he couldn't be long out of Hendon. The rest of the police came out of the side door of the van and stood around, trying to look faintly interested.

'Step out the car, son,' said one of them to me.

What is this – fucking role reversal? He's young enough to be *my* son, the cheeky bastard. What happened to 'sir'? That had soon gone out the window.

They made Mike and me stand some distance apart and different coppers questioned us individually.

'Where you off to?'

I wasn't paying attention. I was more interested in looking at the festering acne that covered the lower half of his face and gave him a cheese-grater complexion. Memories of my own spot-ridden youth flooded uncomfortably back. Clearasil, that's what I'd use on them, I thought of telling him.

He replied to his own question with another. 'Off to the footy, are we?'

Footy? What the fuck is footy? He's been reading too many men's magazines. I bet he drinks Becks out of the bottle.

'Yeah, we were, until you stopped us.'

'Got tickets?'

'No – planning on picking some up at the ground.'

'For your information, the game is a sell-out and I should remind you that it is an offence to purchase tickets from touts.'

Really? I've never heard of anyone getting nicked for buying a ticket.

The copper giving Mike the first degree suddenly became

very animated as he discovered during a body search that Mike rolls his own cigarettes. But although the police found no pot (I bet that's what Spotty calls it), they decided that possession of Rizlas is sufficient grounds to demand a more intimate search. Mike was told to empty his pockets on to the seat next to him. The police officer was obviously disappointed with a threepenny bit, two aniseed balls and a folded-up copy of the *Beezer*, so he then ordered Mike to remove his shoes and socks. Alas, no dastardly weapons secreted between his toes either – just the usual jam.

'Who do you lot support?' asked a more senior policeman who seemed to want to wind this little episode up.

'They're Chelsea and I'm Man United,' answered Mike.

'Come down for the trouble, have we?'

Policeman love using the sarcastic 'we'. They must teach that at Hendon too.

'Go on, fuck off out of here, and if I clap eyes on any of you again today, whether you've done anything or not, I'll nick you. And that's a promise.'

Back in the car, the Old Bill continued to follow us, so we headed away from the ground.

'Drop me off at the Elephant, Dave.'

'Ain't you going to the game?'

'No, bollocks to all this. I'm too old and fat to be running around the streets and swerving Plod.'

They tried to persuade me to go but I'd had enough for one day and, besides, it was ten past three. Off they drove, and I knew they'd be talking about me in the car. 'What's the matter with him? Maybe his bottle has gone.' Maybe it had. I stood on the platform and attempted to gather my thoughts.

I think the bloke in the pub from Hounslow had unsettled me. It was the way he had looked at me. He couldn't handle the fact that I still went and still had the row. Last time he saw me I probably looked like the lead singer of

Chicory Tip, and here I was, a lifetime on, still at it and probably looking more like the lead singer of The Spinners. He wasn't laughing at me but he was shocked. Perhaps I should be like him and distance myself from the middle-aged men who like a row at football. Perhaps I shouldn't. At least we're still living. Putting ourselves on the line. Most of us still look and act young compared to many others our age. But what about Mandy and the kids?

Mike phoned later to tell me that as far as trouble went, the day had been a bit of a non-event. Apparently the police had prevented Chelsea from alighting at London Bridge and had forced them on to a train to South Bermondsey station, from where they had been escorted to the ground. Everyone in the mob had been taken through a special exit gate, so it was a good result for the significant number who were ticketless. There had been some minor scuffles in the ground near the corner flag and after the game the police had managed to keep the rival factions apart.

Some Chelsea boys, though, had slipped the cordon and happened on a Millwall pub in the backstreets. Millwall had come hurtling out but Chelsea had managed to chase them back in, and it seems the windows of the pub had got put in during the mêlée. By the way, the game had ended in a draw.

On the day of the replay, Dave rang and confirmed that I hadn't missed much and said that he agreed with some of my sentiments.

'What are we doing – grown men, with wives, kids and mortgages – running around at football?'

Strange how Dave considered his mortgage to be an asset, or was he lumping his wife and kids along with his mortgage as a liability?

'My running days are over, Dave,' I agreed. 'To be honest, for the past few years I've thought this whole football thing is pretty fucking stupid. Having said that, I still get a buzz going and meeting up with the boys for a drink. But all that travelling up north. Forget it. My philosophy now is, if someone punches me on the hooter, I'm going to punch 'em back. I've had it with going here, there and everywhere and walking miles for fuck all. I've got better things to do nowadays and football is no longer the most important thing in my life.'

Dave had listened patiently to my tirade. 'Pick you up at five, then? It should be well lively tonight.'

'Yep, I'll be ready. Bye.'

As it happened, I ended up taking my own car after remembering I had to work after the game. We arranged to park up where we could and if we got separated to meet up in the Ifield. Now, anyone who has tried to park around Stamford Bridge on a match day will tell you it is a nightmare. Every time I go by car and end up crawling along Townmead Road and squeezing through the double-parked cars in the surrounding side streets, I promise myself never again.

We finally managed to park over at Parsons Green. As we crossed the green on the way to the Ifield, we bumped into a few of our chaps. They told us that fifty Millwall were drinking in a pub up the King's Road.

'Six o'clock and they are on our manor already,' sighed Dave.

As we approached the Ifield, Craig and his pal Terry, a West Ham fan, came out the door looking a touch angry.

'Cheeky bastards!' exclaimed Craig. 'Some wankers in there have asked me to get Terry out the pub because he's West Ham. Some of 'em reckon they remember him from Parsons Green and he was at the front of their mob. He's here because he hates Millwall. No other reason.'

'Come back in with us and we'll try and sort this out,' I said.

In the pub Craig and Terry stood by us and, sure enough, we were approached by a group of Chelsea – some I knew, some I didn't – who proceeded to dig Craig out about bringing Terry. They argued about Terry as if he wasn't there.

'Hold up,' I said. 'What about all the others who go around with our mob? We've had Ajax, Cologne, Werder Bremen from Germany, Glasgow Rangers, QPR, Millwall, Spurs and Arsenal boys with us at different times and no one's said a dickybird. One West Ham fan comes along to one game and you lot take exception. You can't have one rule for one and a different one for another. He's having a drink with us and that's that.'

The boys seemed to take the point.

Suddenly a little geezer bursts in the door and shouts at the top of his voice like the singing telegram boy, 'Millwall on the King's Road! But there's Old Bill everywhere. The area is sealed off. No chance of getting anywhere near them.'

This bloke is almost jostled out of the way by another man, breathless from running, who shouts, 'Millwall on the move! They're leaving the pub!'

It is like the *Titanic* upending. Everyone spills towards the door. Everyone, that is, except me.

'Count me out,' I tell Dave, who knows it's not worth arguing. I say I'll finish my drink and meet him at the top of the road opposite the Gunter. I bet landlords wished pubs emptied like this when they call time each night. Rows and rows of pint glasses and bottles of lager fill the counter, many without a sip taken from them. Who said football fans need a drink inside them to have a fight at football?

'Night, love!' I shout across to the barmaid as I drain my glass.

'Night!' she responds without looking up from the beer-soaked table she is washing down.

Outside the Gunter, I see Dave and the rest of our lot coming up the road.

'Fucking Old Bill have blocked the road and they're using dogs to force us back down here.'

We carry on walking down the Fulham Road towards the ground and stop opposite the forecourt to the Shed. I always feel a pang of nostalgia just standing here. The Shed, birthplace to all of us lot, has been demolished and temporary seating is in place. Millwall have been given the end tonight and by the looks of it there are a few of them walking around the forecourt, openly whacking the odd Chelsea fan here and there. Coming down the centre of the road, bold as brass, are about forty middle-aged men. They are smartly dressed in mostly long, dark overcoats with suits and ties underneath. It looks like an undertakers' convention. They are chinning people in their way but not stopping to look. One bloke at the front, who stands out because he is a fat bastard and is wearing a white trench mac, is laughing as he boots people up the arse in front of him. This is Millwall's young (joke) lot taking liberties.

'Come on, Chelsea, we're here,' announces Fatso.

As if we didn't know. Bosh, and he has taken a nice one on the jaw. Goes down like a sack of shit and the reservoir dogs melt into the moving crowd.

Out of the side streets comes another Millwall firm, also giving it the large one. 'Come on, Chelsea,' invites their spokesman, and they too go down under a hail of fists and feet. Chelsea are everywhere in this forecourt area but are not gathered as a firm and are quickly disposing of anyone who jeopardises their chance of an off with Millwall's main firm. And there is not long to wait. A line of police horses heralds their imminent arrival.

'What's up with that lot?' complains Roy. 'They know if they get off at Fulham Broadway they're going to get an escort.' Bad sportsmanship in anyone's book. What an escort it is too. Horses, dogs, carrier vans and almost as many foot police as the Millwall themselves. At the tip of the procession are about a dozen Millwall who have slipped away from the escort undetected. They are enjoying the best of both worlds.

Winding up the Chelsea but enjoying the protection of the police at the same time. There is the usual old bunny – 'Yer mugs, Chelsea', 'We're on yer manor, Chelsea', 'Where are you, Chelsea?', 'Where's yer famous Headhunters?' and so on. Most people who walk in front of escorted mobs at football are absolute arseholes and couldn't have a row to save their grandmother. Any self-respecting boy would do his best not to get tangled up in an escort and if he did would keep buttoned up.

A few Chelsea lads take leave of their senses and thump a couple of these clowns right under the Old Bill's nose. They are pounced on and carted off straight away. Silly bastards. That is one thing you never do, not in front of the police. Still, it shuts the wankers up and they take their bloody noses and creep back into the security of the escort.

Pat sauntered across the road to stand with us as we watched the Millwall procession. He informed us that this was half of Millwall's main firm and the other half was being escorted down the King's Road. He also told us that a meet with Millwall had been attempted in Wandsworth but they had declined the offer. Meanwhile, the police had managed to place their charge in the Shed forecourt area without any serious wars going off. A few scuffles and a lot of posturing, but that had been it.

'I can't believe that is their main mob,' commented Mike, shaking his head. 'I thought they'd bring a massive mob. This is a poor turnout, isn't it?'

'Years ago they'd have brought a couple of firms both a thousand strong. That was in the days when all the big clubs could muster unbelievable numbers. The recession has even taken its toll on football firms,' I philosophised.

We took up our seats in the West Stand and Millwall were below us on our right. They sang their song about no one liking them and the whole end stood up and joined in. Give them their due, they get behind their team and wholeheartedly support their club, a team that has delivered precious little to their fans and a club that has spent the last forty years trying to disown them.

The match is even at full-time and penalties are needed to decide who progresses to the next round. Chelsea miss one and the Millwall players and fans go garrity. They think they've won the cup. Chelsea take this defeat in their customary gentlemanly and reserved way by throwing anything they can at the celebrating Millwall lot as they spill on to the pitch. We hold back in the stands to allow them to clear so we can have a pop inside the ground. The Old Bill, however, catch us out by letting Millwall straight out the ground. Strange decision, I think, and I'm proved right, for when I reach the exit and stand at the top of the steps that lead down on to the Fulham Road, small fights are breaking out as far as the eye can see.

'Come on, let's get down there!' hisses a voice behind me and there is a massive push down the steps. Those who don't want to get involved stay put, allowing others to tumble past them, content to watch the action from this high vantage point. Out on the street it is very dark and quiet. Ominous and menacing. No shouting, which is a sure sign that both sets of fans are intent on clashing with the minimum of police disturbance.

Mike points over the road where a good Chelsea firm is gathering, with another lot two hundred strong lurking in the shadows of the side road behind them. Then we hear the strains of 'No one likes us' getting louder. Millwall have managed to mob up and are making it known that they are approaching. Roy's brother Andrew tells us that he has just walked along the road with the Millwall and that most of their top boys are at the back because the police are at the front and are attempting to accompany them away from the ground. Then we see the police leading the way and we recede further into the shadows so as not to upset the apple cart.

'Once the Old Bill have gone past about a hundred yards, let's get into them,' whispers someone.

Some of our younger lot have raided a nearby working-man's club and have carried out crates of empty bottles. Those who fancy it slip bottles into their pockets and inside their jackets. Our lot decide to hang back and follow Millwall at the rear. They have no idea we are jammed up behind them and it is all the top faces. Somehow in this melting pot of hate and aggression, we've all found each other. Chelsea stretch right across the road. There is no leader organising us – we're too old for that bollocks. Just the knowledge that any minute now the time will be right for the two best mobs in London to go toe to toe.

Then we hear the bottles smashing and the Millwall lot surge forward. We turn up our collars and pull our hats down, not to hide our identities but because it is fucking cold, and break into a run. It's hard to work out what is going on. Everyone stops and I can just make out a bloke in front of me kicking a low wall, breaking up the loose bricks with his hands and passing the rubble to his mates.

'Here they are!' shouts the demolition man, and only when they all start to lob the half-bricks in our direction do I realise he's talking about us. We go forward at them and it turns into a serious off. The Old Bill are busy containing the situation up the front so this activity at the back is unfettered. I don't feel too old now. If I'm a dinosuar, well, there is a fucking epidemic of them here. Millwall are game and so are Chelsea.

Someone shouts, 'Mind your backs!' and as I turn I cannot believe my eyes. A geezer is wading through the fighting masses swinging a six-foot scaffold pole above his head. I've seen inflatable yellow bananas and hammers at football but this is a first. He runs straight into the Millwall lot, toppling the taller ones and those who don't duck. Even they are not going to argue with this nutter with the bulging eyes and they scatter off in all directions.

A copper on horseback rides between us, forcing a gap between the two mobs. The problem is, when the pole maniac intervened we were all having one to ones, so although two mobs have been parted, we are all mixed in together as the police reinforcements arrive to put distance between us.

A phone tinkles from underneath the clothing of the bloke standing next to me. He rummages inside his jacket and produces a mobile.

'How many of them?' he asks excitedly. 'Right, we're on our way!' He jumps up and down to make himself heard and bellows in his best British Rail announcer's voice, 'Message to all Chelsea fans! Millwall at Parsons Green, and it's going off!'

Everybody jogs off in the same direction. Millwall and Chelsea together, probably towards the green where they can join the others and have the next serious ruck.

On the edge of the green a builder's skip is emptied for ammunition. The Chelsea lot are now carrying wood, piping, bricks and other bits of masonry as they charge on to the green. The light is not good and first of all we charge towards a mob which turns out to be Chelsea. The respite is short-lived.

'Here they are,' says someone, pointing over at the footpath that leads down to the green. Coming down the path is a massive mob. At the bottom of the path where earlier I parked the motor. The motor! It dawns on me that when Chelsea unload the building site on this lot, my motor could well be on the receiving end. In the excitement I've lost our little firm and am standing at the front with geezers I've never seen before, let alone fought alongside. I belt across the green, looking over my shoulder a couple of times to see the two mobs weighing each other up. I get behind the Millwall lot and manage to slip into the car unnoticed. As I adjust the driver's mirror, I can see that sweat is pouring off my brow.

My shoulders are heaving, my chest feels tight and I am blowing out air like I've just run a marathon. All the thoughts and doubts from the previous week race around my head. As I fumble with the keys in the ignition and pull away, I realise I am talking to myself.

'This is fucking mad, this is,' I repeat over and over again.

SEVEN

Stand Up If You Hate Man U

'The fundamental picture reveals that supporters like many of the changes of the past few years. We should take pride in what has been achieved, particularly in the creation of safer and more comfortable grounds and in the ability of English football to attract top-class international footballers. These findings bode well for the future.'

Rick Parry, Chief Executive of the Premier League,
Daily Mail, 12 April 1995

Mandy's doing a quick head count. 'That's it, I think. Two kids, three dogs and two suitcases, three bikes and the pram strapped on to the roof rack.'

Good! At last we can set off on our holiday to Sussex. Not far, but far enough.

Before I can put the motor into gear, there is a tapping on my window. It's my neighbour.

'Off on holiday are you?' I bet he's good at Cluedo. 'Off to Sussex, I hear.' So he knew, so why ask?

'You don't miss a fucking thing,' I reply as Mandy cringes. 'For your information, and that of the rest of the nosey neighbours, we're off to Pagham to stay at a friend's caravan. But I expect you knew that.'

Not put out by my aggressive rudeness, he takes the wind out of my sails by saying that there is a chance he can get tickets for the match next week and am I interested. Am I interested? Is the Pope a Catholic? The match he's talking about is the FA Cup final between Chelsea and Manchester United at Wembley.

'That'll be good.' I smile weakly as he peers over my shoulder and has a good look inside to see what we've packed.

'Good. I'll keep my ear to the ground. I'll let you go then.' He bangs twice on the roof to indicate he is indeed letting us go. Inspection complete. All present and correct.

'Nosey bastard. How's a dope like that going to get tickets?' I say to Mandy as we speed down the road.

'He's only trying to be helpful.'

'He's a typical Man United fan. Probably never been to Old Trafford or even seen United play in the flesh. Watched the European Cup final in 1968 on TV and that was it. Prat. Lives in Surrey and supports Man United. Keep his ear to the ground indeed. I'll fucking skewer his ear to the ground. I bet he's never had a row in his life.'

I glance sideways and see Mandy is rolling her eyes and looking heavenward. 'Trouble with you, Mand, is you never see bad in people.'

'Trouble with you, Mart, is you never see good.'

We'd agreed that we would not mention football or Chelsea on the holiday but, as Mandy pointed out, we'd not reached the end of the road and I was working myself into a frenzy about the final. Two reasons. Firstly, this was the first taste of glory we Chelsea fans had got near for almost thirty years, and secondly, I had not got a ticket. I had missed the legendary FA Cup and European Cup-Winners' Cup finals of the early '70s on account of being too young and not having the financial resources to compete. What was the excuse this time – too old?

Touts were bandying tickets about for around two hundred pounds for a twenty-pound ticket. History or not,

I was not going to line their pockets and swallow that sort of mark-up, although I suppose I knew deep down I might end up doing just that. Of course, the nouveau Chelsea fan would have the Wembley trip well sorted, and that is what got to me more than anything.

I harboured a dream about disenfranchised Chelsea supporters gathering in Wembley Way, our numbers growing by the minute. David Baddiel (a Tottenham fan if ever I saw one) comes marching up from the tube, leading a load of Becks-swilling yuppies towards us. They're swaying from side to side and singing an early rendition of 'Football's Coming Home'. As Baddiel gets level, I smash him in the face and grind his silly little glasses into the bridge of his nose. Frank Skinner's with him.

'Fuck off now, Frank, we've got no problem with you.' But Frank's a bit divvy, as you know, and just smiles that stupid smile. So my mate Roy knees him in the bollocks and he gasps for breath. I see Wedgehead launch Damon Albarn. Phil Daniels shouts, 'But I was in *Quadrophenia*,' and that persuades Time Warp to leave him alone. One of the young ones takes exception to Sir Richard Attenborough calling him 'darling', but Greenaway discards his Zimmer frame and jumps between them, shouting, 'Leave him alone, he's pukka!' We rob their tickets and take our seats next to John Major, David Mellor, Tony Banks, Uncle Ken and the rest of them.

'Where were you at Parsons Green?' I demand to know from Mellor.

'Just outside my constituency, old boy,' he replies facetiously, so I nut him. His glasses break and he falls to his knees. He looks up at me, Piggy from *Lord of the Flies*-style, so I volley him clean in the mooey. Major's bottle goes and he scrambles across the seats to safety. Tony Banks keeps winking at me like he knows something I don't. Only Ken is up for the row.

I'd got the taste for Wembley when the month before we had played Luton in the semi-finals there. To everyone's surprise we won 2–0. I say 'to everyone's surprise' because most Chelsea fans expected us to lose. That was par for the course with us: win or draw against the top sides but then lose to mickey mouse teams. The arrival of Glenn Hoddle, however, seemed to be the beginning of something new. We were playing to form and playing entertaining football at the same time. It was a novelty. There was another surprise about the Luton tie too – their boys were up for it and gave a good account of themselves.

We'd started the day in a pub at Victoria. We'd only just arrived when two vanloads of police turned up and we played out the usual ritual.

'Good afternoon, gents,' said the first one in an exaggerated friendly manner, whilst the other two stood behind giving us the serious stare. Others disappeared into the toilets – looking for what, I don't know. 'Where are we off to today then, lads?'

'Well, first off we thought we'd do a bit of drug smuggling and later on perhaps a spot of gun running, and then if we've got time we might have a bash at some counterfeiting,' replied Brian.

The police spokesman chuckled, whilst the other uniforms made it clear by the lack of any change in their facial expression that they were not amused. 'I think you might be off to the football. Tell me, where are the rest of your motley crew?' Of course, we didn't. They then gathered themselves together, turned and left the pub, huddled into their vans and sped off. Quite what these visits to pubs and their associated banter achieve is beyond me. I suppose it could be argued that they are just keeping tabs on convicted hooligans. Yet many of the thirty or so blokes I was with this day did not have a conviction for soccer-related violence between them.

Manny, who has been going to Chelsea for decades and

still turns up for the big games, arrived at the pub soon after the police departed to tell us that the bulk of the firm were meeting up at Kingsbury, which is one stop past Wembley on the tube. Joined by another wandering group outside, we headed for Kingsbury. The pub opposite the station was overflowing with our lot so we walked down the road a bit and got a drink in there. I'd barely sipped my pint when the doors flew open and another messenger delivered the news that Luton were drinking in a pub just off the Finchley Road. Apparently Luton's boys call themselves Migs (men in gear), and if this was true I couldn't take it very seriously at all. Nevertheless the pub emptied, save us thirty-odd who had just arrived.

'You lot coming?' asked Dave to a row of shaking heads.

'We've only just got here. We're not trekking off back down the line looking for a firm that are more likely not there.'

'But Gregor's just seen 'em.'

Gregor – now there is a name to conjure with. At only five foot tall but with boundless energy, he's known all over London. He's QPR and a comical bastard but he knows just about every firm in London and, for his size, he's game for a row. The Charlie Drake of the terraces, I call him. If there is any likelihood of trouble then Gregor will be there. I can picture him on a Sunday, deliberating over his paper's pools forecast for the fixture most likely to throw up a ruck the following week. He's sucking on his pen. Will it be Swansea versus Millwall or Arsenal and Tottenham? I reckon he's an important conduit of information between the mobs and that is how I expect he met Pat, and through Pat he got to know the Chelsea firm. He started to bring some of the Rangers lot with him and, like Gregor, they were a hungry bunch and made very welcome by our lot. He told me once that the team he hated more than any was Norwich. There is some history between Norwich and Rangers, and I think his ambition is to unite all the London mobs to head eastward and annihilate the capital of East Anglia.

Eventually we left for Wembley, where we spotted a young Chelsea lot giving out some stick to a contingent of Luton supporters moving towards the stadium. Among the Luton supporters were two or three women bedecked in woollen scarves. We could tell they were terrified by the aggressive verbal abuse being given out and we stepped in immediately to defuse the situation. One of the Chelsea boys who thought we'd come to lend support to the bullying spat in one of the ladies' faces and then looked over at us for some kind of approval. My friend cracked him on the jaw and I toe-punted him up the arse. His friends scattered and a nearby policeman dived over and dragged him off without protest. We apologised to the women and assured them that not all Chelsea fans behaved like animals. They were grateful but obviously nervous of us too, which unsettled me.

At the top of Wembley Way the Chelsea lot were milling around, trying very hard to give the impression that they were moving towards the entrances whilst in fact remaining still. We were right. The Luton mob was not off the Finchley Road.

'They're here somewhere,' insisted Gregor, desperately trying to salvage some credibility.

Inside the stadium it was packed. Chelsea took three sides and Luton one, although it looked like they had struggled to sell their allocation of tickets. Chelsea would have taken them, no problem. This is not the final but it is Wembley, and except for some fleeting appearances in cups whose names most people have forgotten, we have not been to Wembley for over a quarter of a century.

So many old faces had turned up I was doing more chatting than watching football. It is at matches like this you find out what has happened to people. People you risked prison sentences with. People you sometimes risked your life with. People you couldn't stand. People who pretended not to know you when it came on top. People you thought you'd forgotten.

'Old ＿＿＿ is a newsreader now.'

As if I didn't know.

'I know. Mandy said to me once when he came on the telly, that looks like ＿＿＿ who used to go to Chelsea. It is, I told her.'

'And ＿＿＿, he's a millionaire now.'

'Yeah, I heard. Bought up a load of council flats from his mum's friends in Wandsworth under the Thatcher thing, let the tenants stay there rent free and then flogged them off for double bubble when they started dying off.'

The boy done well. Lots of them had done well. One of Eccles's old gang I'd seen on the TV now and then. He is a director of a leading media company. One of our lot married a filthy-rich widow and leads the life of Riley. I suppose you don't get to hear about the ones who turned alky or druggie or hermit but, at Chelsea at least, many of the boys did very well and a high proportion became comfortably self-employed. So the theory (that still holds sway in many quarters) that football yobs are of a certain breeding does not hold water: the old man is a drunken gambler; the mother is an ex-fairground boxer with a string of shoplifting convictions; both are on the dole; the eldest daughter is on the game and has three kids by different fathers; and the youngest child is a ten-year-old crack addict. Oh, and, of course, all the children were abused. Although I must admit here and now that I was abused as a child. And what makes it so hard to deal with is the fact that the abuse came from my mother. It hurts, even now, when I think back to those early mornings when she flung open the bedroom door and barged in shouting, 'Get up, you lazy fucking tyke, and get to school!'

The game finished with an easy 2–0 win for the Blues and

the stadium reverberated to the chanting of Glenn Hoddle's name. Never thought I'd see the day when a cult figure from Spurs became the object of worship at Chelsea.

Outside, Gregor and Pat were loitering.

'Chelsea are meeting up at a pub near Finchley Road tube,' Pat informed us. Apparently Luton had been drinking there beforehand and had given word that that was where they would be after the game. Gregor said lots of the boys had already set off. I wrestled for about three seconds with my recent unease about getting involved with the rucks but decided, bollocks, it's not often you make a cup final. Special circumstances. Off we went.

The pub was heaving with Chelsea and there at the bar, heaving more than most, was my food-loving friend Glen. He gave me that special sickly smile of his and said, 'There is a good pub up the road in Swiss Cottage that does a lovely chilli con carne.'

'Leave off, Glen, is that all you think about? And I thought that rumbling noise was the tube.'

I hadn't been with him earlier but I knew he would have already polished off plenty of Wembley hot dogs, burgers and chips. For once, though, we followed Glen's advice because there was no chance of getting a drink in here. At Swiss Cottage we knocked back some celebratory pints whilst Glen systematically worked through the pub menu. The sirens soon made themselves heard above the busy traffic outside and we could see the smudge of flashing blue lights flickering through the heavily leaded windows. It was no surprise that the police and ambulances were heading up the Finchley Road towards where we had been not long before.

'It's kicked off,' said Peter Stevens.

'I wonder what happened,' I mused.

Our answer soon swaggered in through the pub door in the shape of Jerry Kilburn. Never one to cut a long story short, he proceeded to tell us what had happened, switching from an Irish to an English accent as he spoke.

'After you left, someone came in and told us that he had found Luton drinking in a backstreet pub five minutes away. So we went looking for them. Two hundred of us, but the boozer was empty. Then we all went down the tube and there on the platform was Luton's mob. All that was between them and us was two coppers, and one of them was a WPC. They started pulling down an iron roller gate when they saw us and only about fifty of our lot got through. Luton came straight in to them. There was nothing we could do because, for once, Old Bill were a bit sharp. Got to say Luton went for it. Apparently it was their top firm and the fighting was pretty even; it only eased off when more Old Bill turned up.'

That would have been the sirens we heard. It transpired that the police had forced Luton back down one end of the platform and cleared Chelsea away from the area. Kevin, one of our lot, was walking back to the pub when he felt blood trickling down his face.

'Shit, Kev, you've been slashed!' said his shocked mate.

Kevin wiped the now free-flowing blood away with his hand and bent down to look at his face in the wing mirror of a parked car. To his horror, he saw he had been cut, and judging by the smooth, three-inch gash on his cheek, the weapon had been a Stanley craft knife. People used to talk about getting striped years ago but, on the whole, I think it was myth. Now it was happening all too often. Fighting at football is one thing, but no one should have to sport a nasty Mars Bar on their face for the rest of their life for their pains. Pat had been telling me that when Luton had gone to Cardiff in an earlier round, they had taken a good, tight firm up there and done really well. Seemingly the migs were no mugs. Although I suspect that the carrying of knives by their boys could have had more to do with their fear of Chelsea's reputation than anything else.

We found out the next day that we would be playing Manchester United in the FA Cup final at Wembley and I had resigned myself to watching the match on telly. Like I did in 1967 and 1970. But then on the night before the game, down at the holiday caravan, my mobile throbbed in my pocket and it was Muscles, who told me that his old man had got hold of some tickets through someone at the FA. I would have kissed him if he had been with me in person, but fortunately for him he wasn't. He told me that everyone was rendezvousing at a pub called the Lillie Langtry at eleven and that United were meeting in the Black Lion on the Kilburn High Road, only a distress flare away.

'You'll never believe it, Mand. I've got a ticket!'

Mandy did not raise her head from the *Chat* magazine she was engrossed in but just mumbled, 'Really? How riveting.'

The phone rang again and this time it was Dave. Better not mention I've got a ticket, I thought. Don't want to rub it in.

'Fancy going tomorrow?'

'Why, can you get tickets?'

'Got 'em, mate. One for me and one for you. You know the old man trains greyhounds? Well, an owner only walked in the kennels and laid two on him.'

'Unbelievable. Actually, Muscles has just rung this minute and got me one off his old man.'

'No problem. I'll ring Roy and see if he or his brother wants to go.'

'Course they will. Thanks for thinking of me, Dave.' I then filled him in on where and when we were all meeting.

'Another ticket?' Mandy seemed uninterested. 'I don't understand why, if the game kicks off at three, you have to meet at eleven. I hope you're not thinking we're going to be up at the crack of dawn to race home just so you can get there on time.'

'No, of course not. We'll leave tonight.'

Later that night Pat called and told me that Black Willie had a spare ticket for the Olympic gallery. Amazing. Not a sniff of a ticket for weeks and then three of the bastards materialise in a matter of hours. Mandy had a last sunbed (don't know why, seeing as she's African by birth) and helped me load up the car. She doesn't understand football but she's a diamond, that girl.

The next day I practically skip out of St John's Wood station into the lovely sunlight and follow Pat's directions to the pub. When I turn the corner I see that the pub is full and scores of men are drinking and chatting on the greenery outside. Many have taken off their shirts to reveal their fading tattoos and flaccid bellies. The atmosphere is relaxed and celebratory.

I notice Icky politely shaking the hand of one person after another. He hasn't been around for a while and a lot of people are pleased to see him. I reckon he doesn't know or remember half the people queuing to press his flesh but he is too nice a bloke to give that away. Reminds me of Prince Charles at some charity function.

After a couple of hours of solid alcohol consumption, though, talk turns to Manchester United drinking just up the road. Someone shouts to drink up and straight away pint glasses are drained.

'You coming?' smiles Mark as he passes us on the way to the toilets.

'Be along in a minute,' I reply.

Out the window we can see the mob quietly snaking their way across the grass bank and stopping the traffic as they negotiate the main road. Mark, Roy and Dave are up at the front and now Mike, Muscles and I are about twenty yards behind. The pace quickens as we nip down residential roads, through a council estate and a kids' playground. Some cannot resist the temptation to play quickly on the swings. A fat bloke displaying an ample arse cleavage gets wedged on the slide, which prompts widespread amusement and mickey-taking. He has no shirt on and his tits wobble like a lap dancer's as he tries to wrestle himself free.

A heated argument has broken out at the front. Mark, Roy and Dave are telling Frisky, a well-known Arsenal fan and part of Pat's hooligan network, to mind his own business and remember he is only guesting today.

'This is Chelsea, not Arsenal,' Mark reminds the Gooner.

Mike looks behind and is blown away by the size of the crowd. He's seen sizeable firms at Manchester United but even he has to concede that this is the biggest, tightest and oldest mob he has ever been in. As if to underline the maturity of this group, I catch a snatch of a conversation between two fellas, about my age, who are jogging alongside me.

'John – how you doing?'

'Fancy seeing you here, Steve. How are you?'

They shake hands as they run.

'Still living in Ruislip?'

'No, I'm over at Hemel Hempstead now. Where are you?'

'I'm still in Ruislip. I sold your mum and dad's house the other week. Didn't they tell you?'

'No. Really? What, you're an estate agent?'

'Yeah, got my own business. What about you?'

'Still plastering, me.'

I notice they fumble in their wallets and exchange business cards.

An Old Bill van screeches to a halt in front of us but we just swing left and keep going. Kilburn High Road is less than fifty yards in front now. Two more vans appear and police jump out. We simply turn right. We're now three hundred yards from the pub where United are meant to be. Another boozer to our left has the Irish tricolour flag hanging in its window. For the first time the crowd makes a noise.

'No surrender to the IRA!' booms loud and clear down the Kilburn High Road. A brick is hurled through the window and the dinnertime drinkers come rushing out. Our mob rushes them and a few hang around for a good old scrap with the paddies. The rest press on up to the United pub that can now be seen, with hordes of them drinking in the street. We just know that we are going to go through them so easy. But at the next crossroads up riot police dressed in blue helmets with visors and carrying Perspex riot shields come running in from both directions and form a wall to block our progress. The mob stops, causing a skittle effect as people run into each other. No one at the front is going to risk a nicking by taking on the Old Bill so blatantly. More police appear from behind and from other side roads, and they're on a nicking frenzy.

'This is a set-up,' I say to Mike. 'They've thought this one out.'

I see a policeman rip a mobile phone from a man's ear and throw it to the ground, and as the man bends down to retrieve it, he kicks him squarely up the arse. Mike and I dive behind a fruit and veg stall and then walk backwards into a betting shop. We both pull out yellow betting slips from the wall and make ourselves look busy writing out imaginary bets. Two policemen throw open the door and walk in. They study all of the customers and then turn and leave.

'This is like Nazi Germany with the Gestapo looking for Jews,' observes Mike.

Across the street, Chelsea fans are being lined up against the wall. Unlike in Nazi Germany they are not being shot, but frisked and generally manhandled.

After half an hour studying the runners at Sandown but not taking anything in, we ventured out into the street. We met up with Time Warp Terry and a few of his mates from Epsom and jumped on a train to Wembley. We chatted about how fired up the Old Bill were and how we had dodged the indiscriminate nickings. There were some United fans at the other end of the carriage and I noticed them looking down at us. Because we didn't do anything, I suppose, they started to get lippy. They waved us towards them.

'Come on, you cockney bastards! Let's see what you're made of, then,' they said and, to my amazement, they started making their way down to us. Terry's mates didn't hang around and went straight into them. The swaying of the train and the lack of elbow room made fighting virtually impossible but a few punches were getting through on both sides. Mike, being from Manchester, was nervous and didn't want to get involved. I stood there as well, not wishing to offend Mike by clumping his fellow supporters in these circumstances. Anyway, Terry and company didn't appear to be in any danger.

As the train pulled in at Wembley, the fighting spilled on to the platform and Paul Hearne was really digging one of the Mancs out. The police charged along the platform, arrested Paul and attempted to cart him away. We all remonstrated with the officers, saying that the Manchester guys had started it and Paul was just defending himself. The copper did not know what to believe, as he had seen Paul giving the geezer some but here in front of him was a man with a Manchester accent protesting the Chelsea supporter's innocence.

'Let him go,' pleaded Mike. 'I saw it all and this man is innocent. I am prepared to go to a court of law and say so.'

Mike had been watching too much *Ironside*. (By the way, what did Perry Mason do that was so bad he came back as Ironside? I'll have to ask Glenn Hoddle.) The policeman was confused but nevertheless said he was taking Paul to the station for interviewing. Paul was eventually released without charge after he told the police that the Mancs had attacked him in an attempt to rob him of his cup final ticket.

At the top of Wembley Way I spotted Jimmy O'Neill, my United pal from Mitcham. We exchanged pleasantries and Jimmy said, 'You were lucky the Old Bill got there in time down at Kilburn.'

'You're having a laugh,' I protested. 'We had a mob of six hundred and we'd have done your lot, no problem.'

Jimmy grinned and told me not to worry about the sixty or so geezers standing behind him who were giving me the once-over.

'You're all right, Kingy, this lot are with me.'

Skitzy came over and asked me who this lot were. Mancs, I told him out the corner of my mouth. Skitzy screwed anyone who dared catch his eye. Soon more Chelsea had gathered around, interpreting mine and Jimmy's chat as a row in the making. Jimmy began to look a touch uncomfortable.

'You're all right, Jim, this lot are with me.'

At the turnstiles Mike went off to join his lot and we both wished each other's team all the best. Inside, the atmosphere was unbelievable. Both sets of fans were attempting to outsing the other and there was no sign of the hostile regard in which they hold each other. And, for a while at least, we were even steven on the pitch. A shot from Gavin Peacock even clipped the bar, but then the tide turned. A couple of dodgy penalties and two other goals saw us end up losing 4–0. I don't think anyone was too surprised with the result really, although outside the ground people milled around apparently in shock. We knew, though, that this time around the achievement was getting to Wembley and there was more to come. At least, that's what I like to think.

Mike appeared, grinning from ear to ear.

'You were arsehole lucky,' I joked.

'Yeah, it was a close game,' Mike parried.

A fight broke out next to where we were standing. A pack of United fans had picked on a sole Chelsea fan and this was all that was needed to spark a free-for-all. A Manc sneaked up, cracked big Willie on the jaw and then quickly disappeared into the crowd. Willie went berserk. Spinning around, he shouted, 'Who done that? Who done that?' but no one would meet his eye. The police got amongst us and sought to protect the United fans. Our blood was up, though, and some of us who should know better were risking a nicking to continue having a go at them even with police everywhere. A Paki geezer was giving off a lot of mouth and Roy caught him a beauty straight in the teeth.

'That's Dobson from Hayes. He fancies himself as a United top boy,' Jerry Kilburn informed us. Well, there's one for Pat and Gregor's bush telegraph.

The police were intent on moving the Mancs to the station and were not touching us for trying to get at them. A bloke with a thick northern accent burst into song right in the middle of us lot. The idiot thought he was among his own as he rattled on about Chelsea being shit. Until someone got close, hands in pockets, and booted him in the shin. As he lurched forward in pain, someone else volleyed him viciously in the groin. I think he was unconscious before he hit the deck. We screamed at United, as the police herded them in the station entrance, to get off at Kilburn, but they looked straight ahead. I couldn't see this lot getting off before Manchester Piccadilly.

As the escorted United fans filed into the station, there was the usual debate about what to do next. In the event, some went to Kilburn in the vain hope that the Manchester boys would take up the invitation, others went to King's Cross to try and intercept them there, and the rest went back down the Fulham Road to drown their sorrows. Me, I'd been soaked by the rain and was disconsolate at losing the cup. I decided to go home to sulk.

The opportunity for revenge came along sooner than we thought when we drew United in the semi-final of the FA

Cup the following season. The tie was to be played at Villa Park and my mates Stewart and Jimmy Craig sorted me a ticket and arranged a lift for me in their friend's car. As the match was an early kick-off, we set off for the Midlands after breakfast. On the motorway, a giant convoy of Chelsea were Birmingham-bound, many flying Chelsea scarves from their car and coach windows 1970s-style. To my astonishment, we managed to park the car slap-bang outside a pub within spitting distance of the ground. I knew these streets well, having been to Villa and scrapped in these roads a number of times over the past three decades.

In the old days it was also easy to park near the ground, for some reason. Perhaps the locals couldn't afford motors. It was here especially where you'd get approached by groups of young urchins uttering the immortal line 'Fifty pence to watch your car, mister'. What this actually meant was: give us fifty pence and we won't scratch your paintwork. Of course, there was a good chance that even if you did part with the money they would still run a key down the side of the vehicle. But what was sure was that if you threatened them or told them to fuck off, you would definitely get your pride and joy damaged.

The Holte End had changed since the days we cleared it in the '70s and '80s. It was now all seats and we had been designated half the end each. The good feeling we all had about the game seemed justified when Ruud Gullit headed an early goal, but United soon took control again and we ended up leaving the pitch as losers. Below the Holte, a massive Chelsea mob had gathered. There was no back-slapping and smiling and catching up on news. This was the old firm back together and intent on wreaking revenge on United for yet again ending Chelsea's chances of resurrecting themselves in footballing terms. I phoned Mike quickly on the mobile and urged him to get away a bit lively. I didn't like the mood. It was ugly.

Nothing happened in the ground but outside Chelsea fans were stopping cars containing United supporters, forcing them to get out and then mercilessly beating them up. Drivers who made a dash for it had their cars bricked, kicked and battered. Different scale, different war, I know, but I couldn't help thinking about those wretched soldiers in Northern Ireland who accidentally drove into a Catholic funeral and were forced out of their cars and murdered. Mike argued afterwards that Chelsea were bad losers. He was right. Either we had to start winning things or I had to stop going.

EIGHT

The Geordie Yorkshiremen

'At dinner parties, a man can now admit to liking the game without being taken for a neo-Nazi.'
Simon Kuper, *Sunday Telegraph*, 17 August 1997

Days of rain had turned the grass slope at the edge of the terracing of the Holmesdale End at Selhurst Park into thick liquid mud. Me and my mate Steve Wheeler, a Crystal Palace fan, were having a whale of a time sliding down the twenty-foot bank on an old plastic rubbish sack. The game must have been crap because we had stopped watching it and a good number of adults were also averting their eyes from the pitch and looking at us.

Steve's dad had taken us along to what was our nearest league club. Palace were in the old second division and were this day pitched against the equally uninspiring Middlesbrough. Neither side had any players of note. I think Bill Glazier was in goal for Palace and he later went on to play for Coventry City, in the first division, for years. Stevie Kember, the Palace boy wonder, was just breaking through and he too would later play in the top flight – this time at Chelsea, brought in to replace Alan Hudson when he left the club for Stoke City.

What did arouse our curiosity, though, was a group of around one hundred boys and men who had not stopped singing, shouting and generally getting behind their team.

They were Middlesbrough fans who had made the long trip south and we decided to get a close look at this strange race and perhaps strike up a conversation. We tried to open a dialogue but their accents were unintelligible to us. At this time I hadn't really been north of Tottenham and certainly had never had a face-to-face conversation with anyone from the north of England. The only northern accents I'd come across had been on *Coronation Street*, which apparently was Manchester, and *Z Cars*, which was scouse, but this accent was like a different language altogether. The nearest I'd got to this dialect was in the film *Kes*, a tale about a northern kid who kept a falcon. We'd been to see the film at the cinema and it had stuck in my mind for a hilarious scene where a goody-goody kid tries to deliver a message to the headmaster but runs into the school herberts queuing outside the study for the cane. They promptly plant all their fags on the innocent kid and he too gets a whack when the headmaster assumes he is with the gang and makes him empty his pockets. Whilst tears fill his eyes at the pain, the other boys fight to control their giggles.

'Where's Middlesbrough then?' I asked one of the youths. He was tall with an awesome pair of sideboards. I guessed he was younger than he looked and facial hair was still a novelty for him. They were like two hairy triangles stuck on both sides of his face. Here's two I made earlier. People were still wearing burns down south but they had been cut back drastically and sensibly to just below the ear.

'It's in the north-east of England, me old cock sparrer,' he replied in a mock cockney accent. He certainly did a better job than Dick van Dyke in *Mary Poppins*.

'That's better,' I said, looking up at this lump of a teenager. 'Speak like that and I can understand ya. I don't speak Geordie.'

'We're not Geordies,' explained the youth. 'People from Newcastle are Geordies. My town is actually in Yorkshire. I'm a Yorkshireman.'

We carried on the conversation in this manner and the bloke explained where Middlesbrough was on the map. I'd done a bit of geography at school but they seemed obsessed with teaching us that tea got picked in Ceylon and that there were more sheep in New Zealand than people. They neglected to tell us very much about our own country.

He described what it was like up there. Very much how I had imagined it. Factories and industrial chimneys filling the landscape with pungent black smoke; row upon row of dull-coloured terraced houses with no gardens; kids in Stanley Matthews shorts playing football with a sheep's bladder in the street; men sitting outside pubs called the Corner Pin comparing whippets whilst their homing pigeons sit below the table cooing to the sound of their masters' voices. There is no spring and summer, just autumn and winter, and you are compelled to wear a heavy miner's overcoat all year round.

Mr Wheeler, Steve's dad, who had been looking for us among the sparse crowd which was spaced out across the terrace, disturbed my reverie.

'Come on, you pair of mud-larks! How the hell did you get smothered from head to toe like that?'

I bade my new-found friend farewell. Both knowing that the other was probably more or less illiterate, we decided against becoming pen friends. Steve's old man placed his hands in the small of our backs and guided us out of the ground and home.

The perception that northern and southern fans have of each other has been pretty constant throughout the time I have been going to football. We think of them as being years behind the fashion, fat, loud and stupid. They think we are cocky, flash and cowardly. Southern fans have always loved to have a joke at their northern cousins' expense. I wasn't there, but the chaps swear blind the following tale is a true one.

A group of our more boisterous lads were travelling up to Hibernian for a pre-season friendly just a few years back.

Somewhere near the border, they raided a camping and outdoor-activities shop and made off with camping equipment and distress flares, among other goodies. The local police were soon on their case and eventually rounded the Chelsea lot up and lined them up against a fence.

'Right. Which one of you lot has got the flares?' demanded the senior police officer.

The Chelsea boys looked at each other for a few silent seconds before one finally replied, 'Look, I can't speak for you lot up here, but we stopped wearing them years ago.'

It was a good few years before I came across Boro fans again. This time Chelsea were playing up at Ayresome Park, their place, and I travelled up on the special. Times were bad for the team and only four hundred made the trip. The train was split fairly evenly between the avid die-hard fans who attend every game, whatever the weather, whatever the distance (and then assiduously correct the team line-up in the programme with a biro), and us. The mob. As was often the case, the special arrived late. This eased a headache for the local police, as they could escort the visitors to the ground with no interference from locals. Mind you, we ran off a small group of Boro who had been waiting for us as we approached the stadium. The game had already started.

'Let's get in their end,' suggested a couple of the lads. But the rainy, depressing weather, coupled with the fact that the match had kicked off, had dampened the boys' fighting spirits.

'No, fuck it, leave it till after,' responded another, who obviously had a bit more clout. So we stood on the visitors' end and got drenched and savaged by the biting wind. The Boro lot then began to taunt us about getting wet.

Ten minutes before the end, thoroughly demoralised, a few of us decided to avail ourselves of the shelter and warmth of the home end. We made our way down the slippery steps and out on to the street. Glancing backwards, I could see that around a hundred of our contingent had decided to join us. In their end, we paused at the bottom step of the stairs that led to where the Boro fans were standing. They were waiting for us. Looking down, with their red-and-white scarves tied around their necks. Now we knew it was time to buck up and start taking this seriously. We fanned out and walked calmly up the stairs. No shouting. No threats. Just controlled determination.

'Come on, Chelsea! Come on, Chelsea!' beckoned the home fans, although it was obvious that we were indeed coming on. As we neared the peak we leapt the last few steps. We knew they would run. If they'd wanted to get into us they would have come down to meet us. As we swung under the barriers, the Boro fans scattered down the terrace, ignoring the predictable cries of 'Stand! Stand!' from some of their number. We cleared the whole end and then just stood there in the middle, arms folded. We'd made a point. The Old Bill, who had shown no interest up to then, gathered around us and the Boro fans regrouped. The usual face-saving old shit then came out.

'If it wasn't for Old Bill you'd be dead!'

Not worthy of reply. We shook our heads at them and smiled. They knew and we knew.

Two Boro fans wearing Glasgow Rangers scarves and badges elbowed their way to the front and began a dialogue.

'Fucking Chelsea wankers. You're nothing!'

'We must be something – we just strolled in here and cleared your end,' I countered, eyeing their Rangers insignia, 'and, by the way, you may be interested to know that you've just been run by the Chelsea branch of the Hamilton Academical fan club.'

Wembley, in the Datsun Back Light and Tyre Pressure Cup final, was the next time I came into contact with Boro boys.

Dave got me a ticket for what was a sell-out game even though the competition was a two-bob affair. Beggars can't be choosers and Chelsea, at that time, were footballing beggars all right. Our pre-match rendezvous was the Stage Door refreshment post at Victoria. Another Chelsea firm were meeting up at Harrow, and Middlesbrough were supposedly gathering in a pub in Paddington. The rumour machine had it that they were then coming down to Victoria to sort us lot out.

'Let the Geordie bastards come!' growled one of our lot.

'Actually, they are not Geordies. Newcastle are Geordies. Middlesbrough is in Yorkshire.'

The bloke looked at me blankly. 'Oh,' he said, and he swigged from his bottle and walked away.

We stayed for a few more drinks until the bulk of the mob went up to Harrow to meet the rest. We decided to go straight to Wembley. Every station on the way was jam-packed with Chelsea fans. The doors opened and closed without anyone being able to get on or off. The same song was being sung at each station; the underground network reverberated to 'We'll Keep the Blue Flag Flying High'.

At Wembley we were propelled into the human river of bodies flowing up Wembley Way towards the twin towers.

'No sign of Boro,' I remarked to Dave.

'Don't worry about that – they'll be here somewhere.'

Halfway up Wembley Way we were joined by Boro fans, who had just alighted from their coaches. Silly hats and hand-held car horns signified that this was carnival time. A chant of 'Who the fucking hell are you?' went up but the banter was friendly and light-hearted. Pleasantries like 'What's it like to have no job?' and 'Chelsea shit' were being batted back and forth. The police were relaxed as the river ran blue and white and red and white.

By the stadium, we ducked out of the flow and spotted some Chelsea faces hanging around. A scuffle unexpectedly broke out close to the Boro end of the stadium and from around the corner appeared a Boro mob of about a hundred.

'Here we go,' said Dave, rubbing his hands together. 'This is their boys.'

Before we could take a step forward, though, Chelsea were among them – our firm and the day-trippers alike – swopping punches and kicks. Mounted police charged in and dispersed the two groups, with the infantry making odd arrests on both sides to reinforce the message.

'You've got to be a mug to fight outside Wembley,' I mused. 'Old Bill everywhere and the place completely cameraed up.' I pointed up at a balcony below the twin towers. It was full of high-ranking policemen looking down at the operation below. 'Reminds me of May Day in Russia when the army in its full glory marches past the old warhorses saluting them from ahigh.'

'More like those two old bastards on the *Muppet Show*,' said Dave, bringing me back to earth.

The police had moved us on and now we were standing around outside the Boro entrance, busy making arrangements for where to meet after the game. An even larger Boro mob came towards us and was joined by another lot who had, up to that point, been queuing for the turnstile. I could see we were out of range of the balcony and the nearest police were some way off, herding the appropriate sets of supporters to the right gates. It wasn't ideal, but I'm fucked if legs apart and arms outstretched are going to spook me after all these years. And that goes for the others too.

They stopped ten yards from us and started bouncing up and down. Another sign of a mob that is more intent on posturing than doing you any real damage. One of their boys pulled an imaginary knife from his inside jacket pocket and motioned cutting his own throat. Yeah, I get you, it's a game of charades. No speaking, but I've got to guess what you're on about. Right? Like that game on the telly with Michael

Aspel. Don't tell me – I'm Lionel Blair and you're Una Stubbs. Okay, you're telling me that you're going to cut my throat. No, maybe you're going to commit suicide. I'm not sure.

So they've walked over to us menacingly, they've bounced and they've threatened. But because we haven't run, they panic. You've seen it in the playground. Two kids get put up for a fight. One of them doesn't really want to do it but he's not going to let on. He doesn't want to throw the first punch and take the stand-off to the next level. Only when someone comes along and stands in between them does he show any real aggression. The football thug equivalent to that playground mediator is the Old Bill, but they're not here to come between Middlesbrough and us, so it's down to us. We step forward and rush into them. Their front line starts to turn but their blokes behind are pushing them forward. A bald-headed bloke in his late thirties tries to take control. He screams and shouts, 'Stand, Boro, fucking stand!' Unfortunately for him, he is about the only one standing. His face is contorted and blue veins are protruding all over his head. His forehead looks like a motorway map of Britain. He's got more bollocks than the rest of the Boro lot put together. We realise he's going to take at least one or two down with him, so we get busy around him and leave him to abuse his fleeing comrades. It's not fair to do a geezer like that simply because he's the last one left. He should have joined a decent mob.

There is a bit of history now building between these clubs. The previous time the two clubs had met in an important fixture was in the old first division play-offs, when defeat at the hands of Boro had seen Chelsea relegated to the second division. A fairly good game today, culminating in a 1–0 Chelsea victory following a Tony Dorigo goal, goes a small way towards compensating for the previous humiliation. So we are the holders of the prestigious Zenith Data Systems Cup, Zenith Data Systems presumably being a computer company who, in an effort to raise their profile, put their name to this competition. I'm sure it worked. Everyone now knows who Zenith Data Systems are – the company who sponsored that ridiculous mickey mouse football competition in the eighties!

The Middlesbrough fans stay in the stadium throughout the Chelsea fans' rousing reception for their team for winning something (at last) and even applaud our players. They treat their team as if they have won and all credit to them for the way they get behind their players. I can't imagine our supporters would have been so unswerving in their appreciation.

Outside we have a quick check that we're all together and then head back down to the tube. Mark is at the front. Suddenly he turns, faces us and walks backwards, his finger placed over his lips.

'They're Boro, and it's their main faces.'

Word spreads down the line like wildfire. We get level with the underpass for the train station and one of our serious boys taps a Middlesbrough geezer on the shoulder.

'I've got a machete here with your name on it. And I'm going to cut your fucking ears right off,' he smiles as he unbuttons his coat. At that, ninety per cent of them run for their lives. The few who are left put up a spirited fight but eventually retreat behind a wire fence, where they manage to regroup, compose themselves and attract more of their number as they pour out of the stadium.

The police, who could now make out who was who, shoved us lot away and towards the station, leaving Middlesbrough to their own devices. They soon materialised. Down a side road, calling us down. It was double-parked to the limit so there was no room for a good row but nevertheless it kicked off and neither side gave an inch. And what a punch-up! It went on and on and on. The only thing that could stop this fight besides the police would be exhaustion.

I spotted Baldy from earlier having a toe-to-toe with one of ours and he seemed much happier now. Happier that his firm were not bottling this time around.

A police van finally came hurtling down the road, sirens wailing, bouncing from side to side off the parked cars. Protagonists were being mowed down like skittles as others vaulted parked cars to get out of the way. I saw a Boro fan pull a Chelsea bloke – whom he had probably been fighting seconds earlier – clear of the charging van. Out they jumped, no fucking around, trying to arrest anyone. The cracking of wood on bone was all that could be heard. I must say, having been struck by both the old wooden truncheons and the newer springy rubber ones, I prefer the wood.

A few of us managed to slope off and get to the station, babbling excitedly to one another. 'Fucking hell – respect!' whistled one chap, and we all knew what he meant. That lot we'd just had it with deserved respect. They had matched us inch for inch in every department, and they had appeared to enjoy it as much as we had.

But as we stood on the platform, we could see another Boro firm on the train. For some bizarre reason the doors reopened and they steamed straight into us. There were about six Old Bill on the platform and they realised that they didn't stand a chance in hell of quelling this one. They just stood back and screamed into their radios for reinforcements. No chance. The queuing hordes outside would make it impossible for them to get in. Mind you, the half-dozen coppers did get their act together and started trying to force Boro back on to the train. We were only too willing to help and forge a good relationship with the police. With their tacit approval, we punched and kicked the Boro firm back on to the train. Eventually the doors closed and the train was sent on its way. We jumped on the next one, fully expecting Boro to be waiting for us at the next stop. To our disappointment, our train did not stop anywhere, due to a bit of emergency rescheduling between British Transport Police and London Transport, until we reached Baker Street. Some of the more persistent among us went off to Kensington High Street, where it was rumoured Boro had ended up, but we returned to our Victoria base. Eventually Mark, Muscles and the others trooped in.

'Geordie bastards have vanished into thin air!'

'Actually, did you know, technically and historically, Middlesbrough is in Yorkshire, so they're not Geordies at all?'

'Shut up, you boring bastard!'

'Hello, Chris. Martin King here. Can you do us any tickets for the cup final?'

'No chance, Martin. They're going for silly money. Two hundred notes or more.'

'Bit steep, ain't it?'

'Supply and demand, Martin.'

I was having a telephone conversation with Chris, a mate of mine who's now a ticket tout but used to go to Chelsea with the Battersea boys. His main claim to fame was pushing a half-eaten steak and kidney pie and chips into the face of Clive Walker, the former Chelsea player, after a game at Norwich.

'You've got no danger of getting a ticket for sensible money. I'm paying top dollar, and once I've put on a small drink for myself it's ridiculous.'

'Yeah, it must be hard for you to make a living, Chris.'

Chris detected the sarcasm in my voice and said he'd see what he could do.

The phone rang again almost as I replaced the receiver. It was Mike from Manchester. I told him I was not going to pay monkey money for a ticket, so he suggested watching the game in a pub near Wembley. Some of the boys had arranged to meet at the same pub where everyone had met up for the England versus Scotland game. That had turned out to be a right fiasco, with the Old Bill laying siege to the pub and sealing off the surrounding streets. Anyone would have thought that they had discovered Lord Lucan, Carlos the Jackal and a top IRA cell drinking in there together. They had closed the pub and allowed us to leave one at a time. Every individual had had his or her name and address taken, had been photographed up against the pub wall and had then briefly been filmed on video. Our crime? Drinking in a London pub before an international football match. The Football Intelligence Unit definitely didn't have their thinking caps on that day. Because inside that pub were Glasgow Rangers fans, who the police should have worked out were supporting Scotland, drinking alongside not just Chelsea but Millwall, Arsenal, Spurs, Stockport, Oxford, Portsmouth, York, Newcastle and others. There was going to be no trouble and nothing had been planned, but the police seemed intent on raising the stakes. Pissed off at the thought of it, I told Mike I'd probably watch the game in my local pub.

On the day I walked down the road with Mandy and the kids and settled in the local for the build-up. I was surprised just how many Chelsea were here, in this southern outpost, decked out in blue and white. It was another glorious sunny day and Roberto Di Matteo scored before most people had looked up from their programmes. The pub erupted. Eddie Newton sealed it towards the end of the game and Chelsea had done it. We were back. Finally the ghosts of Osgood, Hudson, Cooke and the others could be laid to rest. I kissed the wife and kids at the final whistle and clenched my fists and headbutted the bar as I drank in the euphoria.

There seemed to be a symmetry to it all. I remembered all those years ago losing to Spurs at Wembley and walking out on to the street to face the other kids. I thought about the decline of the club after the FA Cup and Cup-Winners' Cup triumphs, our only remaining pride being our terrace reputation. I thought about the nearly days of Kerry Dixon, Pat Nevin and David Speedie. I wanted to cry. I wanted to get straight on the train and meet up with the boys on the King's Road. We'd done a lot together. Lived on the edge for years. Chelsea's faces, all of them, should be together now. But, of course, they'd be scattered across the country and beyond. My heart told me to get up the King's Road but my swirling guts and head told me to stay put. Since midday I must have downed about twelve pints of Guinness and I wanted to be reasonably close to a toilet and eventually to my bed. The mobile tinkled incessantly as various pals rang to ask where I was. What I was doing. Fuck all, I slurred back to them.

The players came on the box for their post-match interviews. 'Go on, you blue boys!' I shouted up at the television.

A bloke next to me was ordering a drink and I overheard him chatting to the publican. 'That has got to be the worst cup final I can remember,' he said. 'Not very entertaining at all.'

'Why don't you fuck off, you soppy-looking prick!' I interrupted, as the publican winced. '"Not very entertaining"! Well, it was fucking entertaining for me, pal. I've waited twenty-five years for this!'

'Point taken,' said my debating partner and moved rapidly to the other side of the bar. After a couple more pints of the black stuff I was really and truly out the game and I staggered home. Tucked up in bed in my Wee Willie Winkie pyjamas by eight o'clock. So much for partying into the early hours.

I spoke to a few of the boys about the celebrations on the King's Road and around the ground. Roy said by the time he got there the crowds were sitting down in the middle of the road and then jumping up and singing 'One Man Went to Mow'. Good, clean fun, but the streets around the ground were impassable for traffic as men, women and children danced, sang and generally made merry. There was absolutely no sign of trouble until dusk fell, when the police began to gather ominously by the Nell Gwyn and again further down Fulham Road outside Jim Thompson's. Fair enough, Roy thought, perhaps they want to ensure that the celebrations are contained in one small area. But suddenly, hovering above them, was a police helicopter, shining a searchlight down on the crowd.

The row of police had advanced forward from the Nell Gwyn towards the Imperial and it seemed the other column was doing the same in a pincer movement. Why? Dads and mums gathered their children and hurried away. The celebrations were over because the police wanted their fun. Minutes later they had drawn truncheons, charged and tried to clear the area. Let us be clear: this was not a football mob by any stretch of the imagination. There had been no trouble or vandalism. These people were guilty only of extending their celebrations longer than the police would like and blocking a public road with their jubilant celebrations.

But the Old Bill did meet some resistance, because soon all that was left was a crowd of young and middle-aged men who were astounded and affronted by the treatment and who fought back. Some other mates told me exactly the same story. Mike mentioned one guy, overweight and in his mid-fifties, who found himself trying to reason with a policeman. He looked faintly ridiculous in his 1970 Chelsea shirt and a crumpled-up jester's hat.

'What the hell is going on?' he shouted at an older officer. 'Why are you starting trouble?'

'The buses can't come through, so fuck off home before it turns seriously nasty.'

This middle-aged man was taken aback by the copper's attitude and he looked around him to see the crowd beginning to disperse.

'Stay! Stay!' he implored, but to no avail. He then screamed, 'This wouldn't have happened in Eccles's day!'

Roy also confirmed there had been no action as far as meeting up with Boro was concerned.

The following year, after a thrilling two-legged semi-final win over the Gooners, we were back at Wembley, playing Middlesbrough yet again, in the Coca-Cola Cup final. This time the Boro boys had rung and promised to turn out, and they had apologised for their piss-poor show the year before.

Our lot met in a pub just around the corner from the London Palladium and Boro, they promised, were meeting up at Euston station. The game was being played on a Sunday afternoon and when I arrived the pub had only been open ten minutes, yet there were a good hundred faces in there. An hour later the pub had burst its seams and many people were drinking outside. The police did their customary walk through the pub just to let everyone know that they knew that we knew that they knew where we all were. They nodded and smiled at various faces, hoping, perhaps, to plant seeds of doubt among the firm. No one took a blind bit of notice. These days the stakes were far higher than in the '70s and early '80s, and a paranoia about grasses had set in at most mobs. Since the Icky trial, security had been tightened and I would have been very surprised if any police had been able to infiltrate our mob for any length of time. But the worry was, was there a grass? The police knew this and played on it. I doubt there ever was a grass. I can't see what would be in it for anyone.

Some of the boys went off on a reconnaissance but reported back that no Middlesbrough were around. A call came in that they were drinking down the Strand so a couple of lads jumped into a black cab to check it out, but they were soon back without a positive sighting. Whilst all this was going on, I was chairing an argument between Gregor and Stick over who had turned over whom at a recent game between Millwall and Wigan. Stick maintained that Wigan had run Millwall, whilst Gregor (and I was inclined to agree) was claiming that this was bollocks. Gregor told Stick that he hoped he was in Wigan's front line the next time the two teams met. I felt like Kilroy, turning from one to the other and geeing the two of them up almost to the point of fisticuffs. Someone then claimed to have received a call from Boro and said we were to meet them at the top of Wembley Way. The pub emptied and straight away the firm split into factions, taking separate routes to Wembley so as not to put the police on red alert.

At the top of Wembley Way, a good mob of Chelsea had gathered but there was no sign of Boro. The police eventually persuaded us to take up our seats but there was no way Boro would have stood a chance against this firm. We sat in the Olympic Gallery and it was the first time I'd been up there. To be honest, it was like watching Subbuteo, we were so high. I felt a bit detached from the game and the atmosphere. We won again, though, and Chelsea started to sing, 'Can we play you every year?'

Outside, there was evidence of the odd scuffle but no real show. Nelson Mandela said he'd seen a Boro firm picking off pairs of Chelsea and shouting 'Where's yer famous Head-hunters, Chelsea?' but we saw no sign. Queuing for the tube, we all made obscene remarks to a tidal wave of young girls, many young enough to be our own daughters – some probably were – who were walking towards the Empire Pool to see the latest boy band. I picked up on a conversation going on beside me.

'So much for those Geordie bastards showing out this year!'

'Actually, to be a Geordie you have to be born in . . .'

NINE

And Leicester – The Big Baby Squad

'A superbly designed piazza of food courts and themed bus ideas for exhibitions . . . come early, bring the family and spoil them with a good lunch.'

Chelsea Football Club's newspaper blurb about
the opening of the new North Stand, 1994

'Show us your leader!
Show us your leader!'

This was the urgent chant – directed at us – being clapped out by the Leicester City fans one sunny afternoon back in (probably) 1970. I couldn't resist it. Here I was, aged about fourteen, five foot tall and weighing all of about six stone, standing in the gap between the two sets of fans. Both sides roared with laughter as I bowed down Sir Walter Raleigh-style to the Leicester contingent and then milked the applause from the Chelsea boys. Even the police were chuckling.

Chelsea were paying a visit to Filbert Street, home to Leicester City Football Club. All the fans – Leicester and Chelsea – were penned behind one goal, a wire mesh fence separating us. Below us, to our right, was another Leicester cluster, and it was they who were calling for the Chelsea leader to show himself. Leaders were a big thing at the time. The tabloids had been building up the football hooliganism thing and had created some fictional organisers. They weren't really calling it football hooliganism yet; it was all 'bovver boys' and 'aggro' and was still very much tied up with the skinhead cult. One particular newspaper spread had shadowy photographs of so-called leaders at the London clubs, along with dubious interviews and descriptions of the array of weapons they carried to matches. It was obviously a newspaper creation but explained the curiosity of the Leicester fans.

This was only my second trip with Chelsea outside of London and I was lapping up every minute. My first northbound excursion had been to the Hawthorns, home of West Bromwich Albion. Jeff and Tony, my companions this day at Leicester, had travelled with me. The train from London to Leicester had been full and I had even had the unexpected privilege of being plonked in a seat in the same carriage as Eccles, Greenaway and other senior members of the Chelsea war cabinet. They had held a conference across the small wooden table that separated them.

'Right, when we leave the train, everyone stick together.'

'If Leicester are waiting. Then walk to them. No running or charging.'

'When we pull in, no one makes a noise until I say so.'

Jeff glanced at me and whispered in my ear, 'You love all this, don't ya – you little fucker.'

Yes, I did. I copied Eccles's two dozen yes men, who by now had huddled around the seat of power in a rugby-like scrum and were nodding intently at his every word.

When the train slowed, there was a mad rush to pull down the sliding windows and look out. It reminded me of the St Trinian's films, but instead of unruly pubescent schoolgirls hanging out the windows, it was unruly pubescent skinheads. Blue-and-white scarves flew like Christmas streamers in the wind as insults, cans and half-eaten sandwiches were thrown at a gang of surprised British Rail maintenance workers who were working on the track. Someone told me that Eccles's mum made the sandwiches and he made a few extra quid by getting one of his men to hawk them on the train. I was never offered any, nor did I see Eccles take any money. But you never know. I laughed at the thought of Eccles shouting into his kitchen, 'Make us some sarnies for tomorrow, Mum.'

'Sure, son, how many?'

'About six hundred and fifty should do.'

Before the train came to a halt, all but the maturer men were on the platform running, some faster than the snail's pace of the carriages. The chant went up. In those days, when you arrived in another team's town, it was always one of two:

'Chelsea boys, we are here, whoaa, whoaa
Chelsea boys we are here, whoaa, whoaa
Chelsea boys we are here
To shag your women and drink your beer'

or

'Hello, hello, we are the Chelsea boys
Hello, hello, we are the Chelsea boys
And if you are a Leicester fan . . .'

Laughable, really. Many of us on this train would have spewed our guts up if we'd attempted to drink more than two pints of beer, and as for shagging the local women – well, the majority hadn't recovered from the emotional upheaval of their first wank. Nevertheless, the rush you got from landing on that platform, in full song, in a strange city was very special. It meant a lot when you were young and it wasn't bad when you were older either.

The ticket collector retreated into his little box as we

surged through the barriers on to the Leicester streets. A solitary copper with his dog was there to greet us and to my surprise the Chelsea boys obeyed his commands. Not wishing to miss anything, I bustled my way through the mob to the front, with Jeff and Tony in tow. The General and his cronies didn't take too kindly to kids sharing the front line with them. It probably wasn't very good for scaring opponents away, but I was a persistent little fucker and I usually managed to position myself just behind the leaders.

'The park is up ahead!' shouted Eccles, who had obviously been here before a few times. 'Split into two groups. Mick, take a mob around the edge of the park, and the rest of you come with me.'

'That's us!' I babbled excitedly to Jeff.

'Calm down, calm down.'

As if they'd done this a hundred times before (maybe they had), the mob split into two. Quietly and decisively. I would love to have had an aerial view; I'm sure it would have been like a scene from *Spartacus*. We carried on walking behind Eccles across the centre of the park. Suddenly Eccles paused and held his hand high in the air with his fingers wide apart. The mob stopped. Not a word was said. Had he spotted a Leicester ambush gang? Maybe the police? No, he'd stopped us in our tracks to allow a little old lady to put her yapping Yorkshire terrier on the lead and patter off out of our way.

'There's a crew to our left!' shouted someone and, sure enough, walking towards us was the unmistakable sight of a football firm. To their left, though, was Mick and his boys, walking towards them, although they didn't seem to realise, being too focused on us.

'Spread out!' Eccles commanded.

I saw him do this many times after. We fanned out and it made it look like there were more of us than there really were. It was all part of the psychological warfare that the boss man regularly employed. We strode briskly towards them but before we got face to face Mick and his army had punctured their flank.

'Charge!'

Most of them managed to escape towards the metal fence that surrounded the park, with us in hot pursuit. We chased them down the narrow streets, past a hospital, a school and a strange building that I now know was a mosque. Finally the ground came into view.

Wow! I loved this. Here I was, miles from home, tucked between a group of legendary London figures, chasing the local youths across their own town. It is easy to dismiss now how famous these characters were. At school on Monday, were I to tell my classmates that I had spent Saturday after-noon in the Chelsea front line with Eccles, Greenaway, Premo and the Webbs, I would be believed as much as I would if I claimed to have driven the car to the Blind Beggar on the fateful night Ronnie Kray shot George Cornell. There was a clear hierarchy of respect and role models in the play-ground and in the kids' community generally. Everyone looked up to the best fighter in the class, but he would defer to the hardest bloke in the school, who in turn knew his place among the hard nuts of the town. Then, somewhere between the local hard men and the Krays or the Richard-sons (depending on where you lived) came the leaders of the football gangs. Of course, this was a fantasy scenario held only by impressionable young boys who knew no different. Football leaders were never really part of the mainstream criminal culture. Professional criminals and mini-gangsters would regard the hooligan leaders (if they regarded them at all) as harmless eccentrics. Which, undoubtedly, many of them were.

The Leicester fans ran into the arms of the police patrolling the ground and begged for protection. The police pointed us towards a turnstile that said 'Away Supporters' and kept a watchful eye on their local boys as they filed sheepishly into a turnstile only two down that had a sign above it saying 'Home Supporters'. These signs were leftovers from an age, not so long before, when fans could be relied on to police themselves. Not to try and infiltrate each other's space and attack one another. I remember as we queued, the older Chelsea boys were singing across to the Leicester lot:

'Don't go out tonight,
There's sure to be a fight
Chelsea boys are back in town'

to the tune of Creedence Clearwater Revival's 'Bad Moon Rising', which had been a recent hit. Leicester were in awe. You could tell by their faces that they had not seen anything like it. Inside the ground, some Chelsea had got in their pen and proceeded to kick a few arses and run them all over. The police jumped in the ring, rounded up the triumphant Londoners and threw them back in with us. It was at this point that the home fans began to ask to see our leader.

Minutes after my showbiz debut as the young pretender they began to chant, 'You'll never take the Forest! You'll never take the Forest!' This really confused me. I asked Jeff, who was an old hand at this terrace-trouble lark, having been to at least ten more away games than me, what this meant.

'Well, Forest are meant to be the hardest mob in the Midlands, and if they ever catch you they throw you in the River Trent after the match. The police fish you out if you're lucky.'

'What if you can't swim?'

'You drown.'

'What? Have any Chelsea fans drowned?'

'No. They've never caught us, but loads of other teams' fans have.'

Such was my naïvety – or perhaps it was my keenness to believe it – that I didn't question this at the time. How pathetic, though, I did think. It was like getting your big brother on to you. By singing this, Leicester were effectively saying, 'Okay, you've done us, but wait till I bring my brother down.' Personally, I couldn't wait to get up to Forest. Mind you, I wondered what Eccles, Greenaway and company would think about this kid sitting opposite them on the special, grinning from ear to ear with a rubber ring around his waist and wearing inflatable arm bands.

Outside the ground we hung an immediate left and again Jeff, Tony and I had managed to get up to the front. Ahead of us, pouring out a side exit, was the Leicester mob, and before they could prepare themselves Chelsea charged. In our excitement we ran that little bit faster than the rest and we were soon clear out in front. I happened to glance backwards and, to my horror, the Chelsea had for some reason turned right up a side street.

'Jeff, Tony – hold up!' I screamed. The terror in my voice must have been evident because they stopped dead. Leicester, meanwhile, hadn't moved an inch and we were within fifty yards of them. Serious shit. Did they realise we were Chelsea fans? Worse still, did they recognise me from my amateur dramatics in the ground? If we turned and ran, we would have been inviting the worst. We were young and the older ones would hopefully leave us alone, but undoubtedly there would be young ones with them too and they would certainly outnumber us. Necessity is the mother of invention. I called upon my acting skills again and dashed to the hot-dog stall that was situated opposite where the Leicester mob was standing. The others picked up on my plan to fool our opponents into thinking that we were three hungry soccer fans and nothing whatsoever to do with the Chelsea excursionists.

'Three hot dogs, mate,' I puffed, my chin almost resting on the counter as I darted a relieved sideways glance at Jeff. The Leicester mob hadn't seemed to take a blind bit of notice; they continued to look into the empty space where the Chelsea lot had faced them a minute before. They were obviously as confused as we were over the turn of events. All became clear before the man in the white coat had cut the bread roll: Chelsea appeared like galloping horses behind the locals and caught them completely unawares. Startled Leicester fans at the head ran as fast as their legs would carry them, whilst the ones at the back fell into one another.

'Cancel them dogs, mate,' we said, and joined the chase yet again.

Not until the end of that decade did I visit Filbert Street again. This time I was with Babs and the faces that followed him. We had the row in the park and the scuffles in their end but this time the police were more clued up. Back at the railway station, the law had stamped on a fight before it had really got going. I noticed that they were very quick to nick any of our lot but seemed reluctant to collar any of the local lads. Nevertheless, we still went through them like a guillotine, and although they had plenty of bunny, they didn't really put up a show.

Dave Kinshett told me how, after he had done his stint in the US Navy, he and No Coat Les had travelled to Leicester to see Chelsea. Dave had been off the scene for a few years and things had changed. Another mate, Bill, explained to him that football violence was a thing of the past. This was in the aftershock of Hickmott's trial and, for a while, people genuinely thought it was.

Dave listened intently, nostalgia and disappointment welling up inside him. 'I used to enjoy the rucks,' he mused. As if to underline the new order, they walked into a pub where Chelsea and Leicester fans stood drinking side by side. Instead of exchanging blows, they swopped scarves and stories.

'What is the world coming to?' Dave shook his head in a crushed disgust. Inside the ground, they took up their seats. To Dave's bemusement, the only thing separating the two factions was a piece of rope stretched down the centre gang-way. The last time he'd been to a game, metal fences and rows of police three deep had been the order of the day. When Chelsea scored and some fans began to celebrate, some Leicester stepped over the rope and started smacking up some pretty inoffensive-looking Chelsea fans. Nearly everyone in the vicinity climbed over seats and scattered. Dave was horrified.

'Stand! What are you playing at? Stand!'

'Not bloody likely,' replied a yuppie voice travelling fast in the opposite direction past Dave.

'Told ya,' said Bill. 'Chelsea ain't got a mob no more.'

The three of them surveyed the empty seats around them. Outside, the same thing happened, as Leicester steamed into anyone and everyone. Dads with kids. Hats and scarves. Teenagers. Anyone. The Old Bill just stood around and let it all go on. It seemed like these innocent fans were paying the price for the havoc that their wilder ancestors had caused in previous years. Dave stood his ground and clumped a few of their mob. He noticed that they didn't go for him, even though he was in a minority of one, preferring to prey on people who definitely were not going to hit back. Soon other Chelsea fans came and stood by his side, and they managed to get the Leicester firm to focus on them.

'How come you lot never come to Chelsea?' ranted Dave.

He was right. Leicester have never turned up at the Bridge mob-handed. They only ever bring a couple of coaches full of families and friends of the players. Grannies brandishing their knitted teddy bears dressed in the Leicester kit, with their dopey husbands. The sort of idiot who has requested in his will that his ashes be scattered over the Filbert Street pitch. The only younger people on board are the greasy-haired hippy with his bird. He'll be wearing a faded Levi's jacket with silly little badges sewn on and Meatloaf or some such shit written in studs on the back. These people, naturally, were never touched. Yet Leicester treated our equivalents as fair game.

They call themselves the Baby Squad. They christened themselves this following a time when the older faces bottled out of going to Elland Road to play Leeds United. The young boys travelled instead and went toe to toe with the Yorkshiremen. The older lot became known as the Shit-out Mob and the Baby Squad was born. That's the story put about, anyway. They rate themselves, that's for sure. Love getting on the blower and mouthing off to other mobs. They're the wannabes of football hooliganism. But they've never been rated by anyone else, really. A bit of a fucking nuisance, but that's about it. It is hard to show respect for a firm who won't travel.

Just a few years back, Chelsea were again up at Leicester for one of the final games of the season. The Chelsea faces had arranged to have a drink in Loughborough, about twenty miles outside of Leicester. One of our lot received a call on his mobile from a Leicester chap he had become acquainted with through going to England games. The geezer asked what Chelsea were intending to do. Our man told him that they were having a drink in Loughborough and that that was as far ahead as they had planned at this point.

'Stay there, then. We'll come to you,' promised the Leicester voice.

'Fine. We're not going anywhere.'

'By the way, how many of you today?'

Our man did a rough head count and told his counterpart he reckoned about a hundred. The line went silent for a minute but then the Leicester man signed off, saying they'd be there within an hour. Everyone tensed up. Game on.

Most people drank slower. A few threw back as much as they could, for Dutch courage, without drawing attention to themselves. Conversation was stilted. But ninety minutes passed and still no show. Chelsea pressed redial.

'Where the fuck are you?'

'Two of our lot are on the way over to talk to you.'

'Two of you! To speak to us! I thought we was having a row, not a fucking coffee morning, you mug!'

A mini-cab duly pulled up outside and two of their firm cautiously stepped out. Our man in command today, the man with the mobile, walked out to greet them. 'All right, chaps?'

Fear was etched all over their faces.

'Don't come into the city centre. It's crawling with Old Bill.'

'But I thought you were coming over here.'

'Yeah, we will. We're not going to the game. Soon as the Old Bill fuck off we'll be straight back.'

'You could have rung and told us that.'

The Leicester spokesman couldn't really explain himself but he didn't seem too interested. He kept peering into the pub over Tony's shoulder, attempting to weigh up the opposition. 'Any of the Combat 18 boys with you?'

'Definitely. They're all here, all right. Along with a few Liberal Democrats, some Socialist Workers and a bunch of Young Conservatives.'

'Righto.' He nodded vacantly and the two of them climbed back into the cab and sped off. They love a legend, this Leicester lot. Twenty-five years ago they're asking to see our leader because they've read a lot of cack in the newspapers, and now they're wanting to see the famous Combat 18, who the press have decided are synonymous with the Chelsea Headhunters.

One of the young Chelsea firm was straining at the leash throughout this little episode 'We should have cut 'em and sent 'em back in the cab caked up with claret.' He'd have done it, too, as he'd already established a reputation as being a bit reckless with a blade.

'Fuck this,' declared Dennis, an older hand. 'They ain't

coming back. If they was coming, they'd have come. Those two were just a pair of nosey wankers. Two bob Leicester as per fucking usual.'

'Just goes to prove they won't come out of Leicester, even to here, let alone London. I'm going to the game,' volunteered someone else. Half the firm seemed to agree that a rendezvous was highly unlikely and they drifted off to the game. The other half sat tight in the pub. Not so much in expectation but because they didn't have tickets and couldn't be arsed anyway.

The game ended and still fifty Chelsea sat in a Loughborough pub twiddling their thumbs. The phone came out again.

'You lot coming, or what?'

All niceties have been dispensed with now.

'We ain't coming.'

'What d'you mean you ain't coming?'

No reply, just deafening silence.

'They ain't coming!' shouted our man to the rest of the mob, who immediately crowded around the phone trying to grab it as if the Leicester firm resided inside the handset.

'Fucking wankers!'

'Bastards!'

'Right,' announced our main man. 'If they won't come to us, we'll have to go to them.'

That was it. If there was one thing this Chelsea firm could not abide, it was bad manners.

The cream of the '90s Chelsea firm alighted at Leicester station a good hour after the game had ended. Most Chelsea followers were relaxing in their coach, car or train seats well on the way back to London now. Adjusting their headsets in preparation for a dirty video. For this lot, though, the day's climax was still to be reached.

Turning left out the station, they spotted a crowd of people at the top of a slight hill.

'That's them,' decided Nick from Bromley. Chelsea ambled up the hill towards them and Leicester looked on.

At fifty yards, Tony issued an instruction. 'Wait until we're in amongst them and then pay them.'

'I don't think so,' chirped one of the lads at the back. 'Take a look behind.'

Coming up the hill, in full flight, was a hundred-strong gang.

'It's not us,' observed Roy.

Within seconds Chelsea were overwhelmed from the front and back. The only thing to do was fight like crazy. There was no escape. Fortunately Chelsea managed to back themselves up against a wall, which helped but only strung out the punishment that was being dished out. Chelsea's top firm had been caught out by the slimiest mob in football. As the blows rained in, claret was flying off one geezer's head on to the bloke next to him. It was only a matter of time before someone got badly hurt. A lone copper arrived and, give him his due, he threw himself between the two warring mobs. Chelsea used this respite not to retreat but to launch back into the locals and this time they started to get the upper hand for the first time. Finally, police reinforcements turned up and prised the mobs apart. The police helped one of the twins from QPR to his feet. He had been dragged behind a car and savagely beaten. They were concerned that he had broken ribs and had suffered serious concussion. Eventually a limping and bedraggled group of Chelsea fans were escorted back to the station. Leicester disappeared into the evening air.

On the platform the Leicester Old Bill lined everyone up and one of their number scanned up and down the line with his camcorder. Fulham Old Bill turned up. They seemed angry that Chelsea had allowed Leicester to turn them over.

'Are you lot mad? We've just done a head count and there are twenty-seven of you lot. Our guess is there was easily a hundred in their mob. What are you – kamikaze now?'

At this point a local train arrived and the two Leicester jokers from earlier in the afternoon stepped off.

'We've been looking everywhere for you lot,' declared the only one who seemed capable of talking.

'Don't worry about that. We found your lot. We bashed 'em right up,' interjected Roy, who, had the Old Bill not been around, would have given these two a right larruping. The officers from both forces put us on a train and rode shotgun home with us. At every stop more police lined the platforms. This was real VIP treatment.

On reflection, most of the boys agreed that going into Leicester had been a bad decision. Twenty-seven, no matter how game, cannot take on such a huge mob and expect to come out on top. Leicester had bottled from coming out to Loughborough and that should have been enough. They had lost face, not Chelsea. It was this incident that set the tone for future relations and as I write, with the exception of Spurs, it is the Midlands club that excites hatred in Chelsea more than any other.

Not too long later, the two clubs were drawn against each other in the FA Cup, with the game to be played at Filbert Street. Chelsea took up their full allocation of tickets. Fifty of our lot who had travelled up on a coach clashed with a similar number of Leicester outside the ground and ran and battered them all over. However, twenty or so lads had bought tickets for a section of the ground which was not only among the home fans but also a long way from the Chelsea contingent. They were seated by the corner flag and as Chelsea were soon 2–0 up they became quite conspicuous by their celebrations. Zola came close to take a throw-in and an Asian fella began to abuse him.

'Fuck off back to Italy, Zola, you wanker!' he screamed. 'It was your goal at Wembley that fucked us up, you bastard.'

'I don't remember Italy playing Pakistan at Wembley,'

parried one of our lot, and at that it kicked off. A few Leicester came menacingly over the seats but were easily repelled. The patriotic Asian Englishman and his friends made themselves scarce but the fighting continued intermittently for some minutes. This game was live on TV and fighting at football matches didn't happen these days, especially in all-seater stadiums. The commentators were taken by surprise and forgot to mention it. For a minute the cameras drifted over to the action off the field. The stewards didn't want to know so a few police were located, and they eventually led the Chelsea away down the edge of the pitch.

'There is no room in the Chelsea end so unfortunately we are going to have to chuck you out,' smiled one officer. 'But if you leave quietly and behave yourself, one of my colleagues will escort you to a pub where you can watch the rest of the game on television.'

A policeman took them to a pub which was near-empty save a few bouncers who had presumably been hired to look after the premises in the busy periods before and after the game. He had a quick word with the landlord and left them to it.

Fifteen minutes later, a fella walks in, has a look around and leaves. Outside the boys see him pull out his mobile and make a call.

'They're coming,' says Gareth. 'He's calling for reinforcements.'

'You're getting paranoid,' laughs Tony.

But Gareth is right. Minutes later a brick comes hurtling through the pub window and the front door explodes. The bouncers, who only minutes before looked like they'd be happy to give Mike Tyson a good row, jump the bar and disappear. The landlord grabs the till, cradles it in his arms and follows. World War III has broken out. Anything portable is used as a missile. Ashtrays, glasses, chairs and tables fly through the air. The glass in a fruit machine shatters and money clatters on to the threadbare carpet. A Chelsea fan kneels down, one eye on the battle and the other on the change he scoops into his pocket. The pub is pretty much demolished as Chelsea successfully prevent all the Leicester mob getting in – but not without casualties. The projectiles have taken their toll on a number of boys on both sides.

The police arrive with a couple of ambulances in tow and they help the more seriously hurt to their feet. The damage and injury that can be caused in just a few minutes is shocking to all. The situation is clear. Chelsea are in a pub. A pub where the police have put them, and that pub has now been attacked by a large Leicester mob. People have been hurt and property extensively damaged. The Leicester mob have made no attempt to flee and have stayed to observe and relish the aftermath.

'Ain't you going to do fuck all then?' demands one Chelsea boy.

'Can you identify your attackers?' counters one of the policemen.

The Chelsea fans just smile at the cynicism of his reply. The attackers are clearly all standing alongside the police.

The game had ended in a 2–2 draw so the replay at Chelsea promised to be very interesting. Leicester's firm, in their book at least, had notched up a couple of results against Chelsea, so surely they'd now make the trip? Dave arranged to pick me up in the afternoon, although it was an evening kick-off. Anticipation and excitement were high. It had been a reasonably quiet period on the trouble front as many of the mobs had given up travelling. Leicester may be unethical, but at least they still had a firm and they had promised to turn up.

We went in a pub on the New King's Road and were having a good piss-up, partly because a lot of the old firm were here to even the score with Leicester and partly because it was my birthday. Mike from Manchester called on the mobile. I told him that a lot of the lads had gone over to Bethnal Green looking for Leicester. This was another sad thing about this star-struck firm. When they did come to London, they always plotted up in the Blind Beggar in Bethnal Green. The Blind Beggar has gone down in history because it was there that Ronnie Kray shot and killed George Cornell. Leicester obviously got some sort of kick out of leaning up against the same bar or pissing down the same urinal as Britain's favourite gangster. Surprise, surprise, they weren't there anyway.

By six the small firm had returned from the East End and our pub was chock-a-block. Talk of revenge floated across the bar. Another rumour started flying around that Leicester were drinking in a boozer down at South Ken. A posse was dispatched to check this out. Mobile phones tinkled away as the tension mounted. News came back that no Leicester were to be seen. The Cry Baby Squad had ducked out again. It was a good job for them, because I don't think I've seen a group of people so keyed up for revenge in recent years. We didn't even bother going to the game, preferring to sit in a Greek restaurant around the corner from the ground and watch the match on Sky.

We won courtesy of a penalty late in the game and as soon as that was put away we marched around to the ground hoping to run into someone. Some of us made our way into the away supporters' section of the East Stand and wandered around looking for some likely suspects but there really was no one around. Some of the lads even boarded the Leicester coaches and walked up and down the aisle looking for someone to whack. Someone they recognised. Someone who got trappy. No danger. Leicester's one hundred per cent record of not turning up at Stamford Bridge was intact.

Okay, I'll admit they did make a show of sorts at the league game at Chelsea later that year. About ten of the boys had again been halfway around London trying to hunt down the elusive Leicester firm. They had decided to give the game a miss and were drinking in the White Hart opposite Fulham Broadway tube station when a forty-strong Leicester firm emerged nervously from the station entrance.

'Game on,' said someone as the Chelsea group tucked themselves quietly behind. A friendly introduction several seconds later was sufficient to send half of their boys scattering, but the remainder turned around to fight. The first punch sent one of the lard-arses clattering to the deck and then they all bolted. Most made it back into the relative safety of the station but a few took the sort of spanking that big babies deserve. They were spared serious damage by the boys in blue, who got to the scene all too soon.

Revenge of sorts had been exacted, but no one was kidding themselves that the score had been settled over the early-evening ambush in Leicester a while earlier. Obviously the game at Filbert Street the following season was marked down as a key fixture in the firm's season. Two hundred made the trip from London and the Football Intelligence Unit saw this as a good opportunity to update their database. Before boarding the train, everyone was subjected to a stop and search and asked to provide a name and address. Fatuous, really, as Fulham Old Bill could have produced a register and merely ticked off the names as they arrived. Strange that in an age of relaxed border controls between European countries, some classes in Britain experience problems crossing from one English county to another.

At Leicester station more police were waiting to greet Chelsea and insisted on a second dose of name-taking. It was noticeable that the Fulham police were not too keen on this intervention from another force. Chelsea were then escorted to a pub that the police had pre-arranged for them. There was a strong suspicion that the boozer was wired up to the eyeballs and conversation was therefore muted. Careless words cost, and all that. Video cameras whirred away and a not-so-plain-clothes policeman dressed up in an army camouflage suit took reel upon reel of still photos.

A police inspector entered the pub and informed everyone that those with tickets would be escorted to the ground for their own safety. This was greeted with loud jeers.

'Think we can't have a row then?' shouted someone from the back.

'On the contrary, I'm sure you can,' replied the inspector, whose accent suggested a public-school education. He must have failed at something else to have ended up in the Old Bill.

'Those of you without tickets can continue to drink in this pub until the end of the game, when we will accompany you back to the station.'

At this the pub emptied and everyone attempted to make their way to the ground. Mounted police and dog-handlers got around us, only allowing more cameramen space to film our progress. At a crossroads a large number tried to turn left but the police were having none of it. However, in the ensuing mix-up, a few did slip the escort and a dog-handler, on seeing this, leapt from his vehicle, grabbed his dog and gave chase. One opportunistic Chelsea chap doubled back, opened the door of the van and released the handbrake. It didn't even need a shove; the van rolled down the hill, picked up some speed and ended up embedded in the side of a police squad car to widespread cheers and applause. Even some of the coppers in the escort had to stifle the urge to laugh. The red-faced dog man didn't see the funny side, though.

Everyone was cheered further when word came through that the few Leicester boys who had been collared for the little spat near the White Hart the previous season had been in court and had been dealt with. They had been found guilty on three counts: having insufficient bottle, desertion in the face of the enemy and failing to appear at Chelsea for the past thirty years.

TEN

European Harmony

'Margaret Thatcher believed that football fans were the second enemy within and she handed control of policy on football hooliganism to a group of ministers who knew nothing about the game, according to Kenneth Clarke, the former Chancellor.

'"Someone took her to see a game in Scotland once and whether it was the songs the crowd sang or something else, it had a marked effect on her. When she discovered that any of her ministers went to football regularly, she wondered why we were joining this band of hooligans. She kept on considering policy on football hooliganism with a group of ministers advising her, whom she relied upon but who had never seen a football match in their life."

'Mr Clarke, who has supported Nottingham Forest for fifty years, was excluded from any advisory role on football policy.'

The Guardian, 12 January 1998

Following Chelsea's 4–0 hammering at the hands of Manchester United in the FA Cup final, a sojourn into Europe was probably neither expected nor deserved. Yet United managed to win the double, thus allowing Chelsea entry into the European Cup-Winners' Cup by the most tenuous route.

CZECH MATES

The first round promised to be pretty uneventful, with Chelsea being drawn against a Czech team that few had heard of. A 4–2 home win set us up nicely for the away tie. Quite a few of the lads and Chelsea die-hards made the trip to the former Communist country. Icky even made a guest appearance and by all accounts he was his old self, dashing around organising tickets for the game. Although his trial, his imprisonment and the subsequent quashing of his sentence were ten years ago, his presence – or alleged presence – at games excited the tabloid media like no other. Some time before the Czech match the *Today* newspaper, which prided itself on being a cut above the *Sun*, *Mirror* and *Star*, its tabloid stable-mates, devoted its front page to a colour picture of Icky being deported from Norway on the eve of an international match. They sneered at his claim that he was only selling T-shirts, but he was. The point is – what is a half-serious newspaper doing splashing pictures of Icky on its front cover? He was not found to be smuggling in any heinous weapons. No poison gas or grenades. He did have a quantity of cotton T-shirts in his holdall though. The fact was that he was a convicted football hooligan who had been sensationally jailed some years earlier but who had been, much less sensationally, freed and compensated shortly after. How could he warrant such media attention? Why would newspapers be on his case in such a way? One can only conclude that an institution with a grudge against Hickmott must play a part in keeping the legend alive.

More recently, when Italian police stormed innocent England fans at an international tie, one of the papers managed to spot Icky in the crowd. The next day his face was ringed and plastered across the papers, the inference being that in some way he had orchestrated the trouble. The fact he was standing some distance away from the fracas and appeared to have his eyes fixed on the game made no odds. More relevantly, perhaps, the great and the good who attended the game were unanimous in their opinion that England fans had been indiscriminately attacked and mistreated by the police throughout the day. Radio shows and newspaper letter columns were full of it for days.

Just before the 1998 World Cup finals the papers were at it again, with one of them publishing a rogue's gallery of 'twenty thugs who must not be allowed to travel to France'. Icky, naturally, was prominent and they used the picture of him spectating at the Italy match. I think they called him the General. They call everyone the General, always have.

I sometimes wonder why Icky does not resort to the law to stop these regular slurs on his character, or at least correct the cuttings-library allegations that are trotted out in the media time and time again. But I suspect he is a pragmatist. He knows how the British law and media work. He knows that any legal victory would only come at a lifetime price of harassment and restriction of movement.

Get off your soapbox, I hear you sneer. The man is a football thug and it's tough luck. My point entirely. Icky was no angel, but he's no Fred West, Ronnie Kray or even Ronnie Biggs. Imagine his conviction was not for football violence but for some other criminal offence. Imagine he was black. See what I mean? He would be a *cause célèbre* before you could say Blair Peach. I'm not really trying to make a political point here but I am trying to illustrate the ridiculously disproportionate interest shown by media and law-enforcement agencies in football violence and football hooligans.

One final observation on that Italy–England match. I was on holiday in a sleepy Norfolk village with the family and I went down to the local to watch it on the TV. It seemed the entire village had turned up to support their national side. Men, women and children. Pipe smoke and brown ale. As the events on the terrace unfolded, it became clear that the

English fans were being subjected to a vicious and unprovoked assault from the baton-wielding Italian police. The mood changed from 'here we go again' to shock, then to anger.

'Run back at them – they'll only surrender!' shouted one old-timer.

'Put your truncheons down and fight like men!' remonstrated a woman.

'Come on, England, you can do better than this!' This was from a young man in a three-lions shirt. Every surge back by the English was greeted with excited encouragement. Not once did I hear any complaint about 'bloody English hooligans'. I recount this story only to illustrate that 'ordinary people' do not necessarily hang their heads in shame at the sight of English fans abroad. In fact, when the chips are down, the masses are as likely to throw down their briefcases or tools and join in as they are to condemn them.

Going back to the Czech game, my man in Prague told me that for some reason they had switched the fixture away from the capital to a venue across on the other side of the country. The night before the game, a large group of Chelsea gained entry to the local nightspot following a long pub crawl. All went well for a couple of hours but then the inevitable brawl broke out between a bouncer and a Chelsea boy. It became a free-for-all and the club got wrecked. The fighting spilled out on to the street, where most of the bouncers took a hiding and ended up spark out on the floor. Except one. He was six foot six and judging by his movements was a martial arts expert too. No one could get near, and those who tried were swiftly launched or put on their arse. He could not be budged. They hit him from behind with bottles and chairs, but he never wavered. By the time the Czech police arrived he had six swarming all over him but still he did not succumb.

The six, along with some others, were bundled into a van

and delivered to the local nick. They were a shade nervous. Okay, it wasn't *Midnight Express* territory, but they didn't expect to get read their rights either. But after a couple of hours banged up they were informed they would need to pay a fifty-pound fine each and they would be released. All the fellas coughed up and left the police station to rejoin their party.

'That's how it should be in England,' decided Steve, one of those who had been arrested. 'It would save money on all those undercover operations and camera kit. No paperwork. No court. You've just got to come across with the readies. A sort of pay-as-you-row.'

On the day of the game, more and more Chelsea fans arrived in the town centre. The bars were full of largely good-natured Englishmen. At one stage fifty Czech skinheads materialised in the town centre. They wore the green or blue flight jackets much favoured by young men in England in the '70s and '80s, the ones with the orange lining. They were up for a fight and walked menacingly over to the largest group of Chelsea who were milling around the street. When our boys just stood and laughed at them, they realised that the Englishmen were not about to run. They resorted to gesticulating and chanting, but all this did was make Chelsea laugh even louder. The Czechs seemed genuinely insulted and ran into the Chelsea, threw a few furious punches and ran straight off again.

More and more Chelsea turned up, many arriving by taxi. The drivers must have thought all their birthdays and Christmases had come at once. The Czech police were laid back and merely looked on quizzically as the Chelsea fans drank themselves stupid. But when some officers from the Football Intelligence Unit turned up, the atmosphere began to turn. They immediately got the video cameras out and darted around taking still photos of all sorts of individuals. They began to point out known fans to the Czech officers, who in all honesty didn't appear interested. The game ended in a bore draw, but it was enough to see Chelsea through to the next round. The Czech skinheads reappeared after the game but were soon dispatched after a scuffle in the town centre. All in all the Chelsea fans who had made the trip concluded that the Old Bill had been fair and the people friendly.

The next round saw Chelsea drawn against Austrian Vienna, or Memphis Vienna as they became known once a tobacco company had started sponsoring them. The first leg was a goalless draw at the Bridge and the return finished 1–1, Chelsea going through on the away-goals rule. A legendary John Spencer solo effort had done the trick.

BRUISED IN BRUGES

Beautiful Bruges was the venue for the next round. Excitement was now high, as a European trophy for the Blues began to look a real possibility. Literally thousands of Chelsea attempted to make the trip but were on the day prevented from travelling in their hundreds. At Ostend it didn't matter if you were drunk or sober, black or white, old or young, male or female; if the Belgian customs officials didn't like the look of you, that was it, back to England on the next ferry. What happened to freedom of movement within the European Union? I mean, we're happy to let anyone in our country, from Nazi war criminals to Serbian gypsies – and they're banking on staying! Seeing that the hysteria surrounding the fixture was reaching boiling point, I elected to stay put for this one.

The night before the game the Chelsea fans were well behaved and could move freely around the old city. The day of the game was the same, with the police maintaining a low one, but in the late afternoon, for no apparent reason, the tactics changed. Water cannons were wheeled out on to the street and were used on Chelsea fans drinking in the open outside a bar. Their only crime was not progressing towards the ground at the pace the police would have liked. Military-style helicopters hovered overhead and police dogs were allowed to run loose and snap and bite innocent people walking towards the stadium. Then an indiscriminate rounding-up of fans took place. People with and without tickets were herded together, put on buses and taken to huge empty warehouses some distance from the ground. They were imprisoned overnight with no toilet facilities and no food or drink before being released in the morning without so much as an explanation, let alone an apology. If only the Belgians had shown the same determination, resilience and tenacity against Hitler that they did against women, children and inoffensive Chelsea supporters that night, history might well have told a different story.

Muscles' account of his experiences that day are probably pretty typical. He and about fifty others had enjoyed a cultural evening in Brussels the day before the match. The following morning they had been up bright and early and had taken the train to Bruges. The train they were on pulled in just behind another that was full of Chelsea and they noticed that as the fans disembarked they were immediately surrounded by police and marched off to a 'holding' centre. On seeing this, Muscles and company sat tight until the coast was clear.

Well pleased they had managed to evade capture, they soon had the smiles wiped off their faces when only a hundred yards away from the terminus they were confronted by one policeman and his dog. He told the boys they were under arrest and marched them across the road into a car park. From here he radioed for a coach to collect and deliver them, presumably to another temporary prison. This provided them all with a pleasant interlude, because when it arrived the coach turned out to be in the hands of the world's worst driver. He took half an hour to reverse into the car park and succeeded in denting the gate, hitting a lamppost and tearing his bumper off in the process. Whilst this Belgian Frank Spencer was negotiating the vehicle backwards, one of the boys noticed a wooden gate at the side of the enclosure that led out on to the road the other side of the six-foot brick wall. As the policeman and driver combined their organisational and driving skills, the boys slipped out, shutting the gate behind them.

Dave recounts another story, which I have heard a few times since, including at the France World Cup in 1998. An English camera crew entered the bar in which they were drinking and singing and chatted them up. The crew eventually suggested that if they would like to go out into the street and lob bottles at passing home fans and allow them to film it, they would be all right for drinks at the bar. The boys agreed and stepped out into the daylight with the smiling camera crew.

'Where do you want us?'

'Oh, just do what comes naturally,' replied one snide member of the film crew with a sickly smile.

The TV people cranked their cameras into action and raised their furry microphones aloft. The boys promptly brought their bottles, glasses and feet down with force on the expensive camera equipment and smashed it all to bits. They then proceeded to chase the frightened crew across the square. The main cameraman dropped to his knees, trying to protect his precious equipment, with tears rolling down his cheeks. The Chelsea boys walked back to the bar away from this strange sight.

'Must have been freelance,' someone observed dryly.

Another story doing the rounds was that the TV presenter Matt Lorenzo had been attacked in his hotel room by hooded thugs (that's what the TV said). He was said to have been punched and kicked as he replied to a knock at his hotel door. Very strange. Now who'd want to do that to nice old Matt?

This game was one of the few attended by co-author Martin Knight in the '90s; his account follows.

* * *

I'd barely set foot in Stamford Bridge for twenty years and matches I did attend were normally by accident rather than intention. But, like thousands of dormant (or fair-weather) Chelsea fans across the country, the Bruges fixture temporarily reawakened the Chelsea bug dormant inside me. My long-standing pals Pete, Pommy and Woody all decided to make the trip too. We drove to Harwich, where we figured the police wouldn't be so sweeping in their refusal to allow Chelsea supporters to travel. The police were there but seemed good-humoured and we only saw them refuse passage to a small group of fans who were clearly pissed.

On the ferry the main bar was full of Chelsea and I scanned the faces, hoping to renew acquaintances from the '70s. There were plenty my age but none I recognised. We took a table in the corner and were eventually joined by three lads from Basildon. We started to sink the Stella and everyone seemed to come up on the alcohol at the same time. The barman stuck on a Madness tape and someone shouted at him to turn it up. As Suggsy went into 'My Girl's Mad at Me', the whole boat joined in. That was a wonderful moment: two hundred men united in song as a bolt of nostalgia coursed through their veins simultaneously.

The Stella kept flowing and we fell into a game of cards with our younger friends from Essex. Drinking and playing cards with strangers rarely go well together, even if you do support the same club. We were playing nine-card brag and the kitty kept building; when Woody scooped up the substantial winnings, they didn't like it. The eldest one of the three had become quiet and I noticed him looking at me a lot. When someone suggested we play something called bastard brag (a strange game that involved putting a single card on your forehead), he exploded.

'That's an Old Bill game! You're undercover Old Bill, you are!'

His accusation was directed at me and he pushed back his chair, in preparation, I thought, to fly across the table at me. Now, at five foot five and noticeably out of condition, I think I make an unlikely copper, but the tape had finished, the deck was silent and two hundred pairs of eyes were fixed firmly on our table.

'I'll give you fucking Old Bill!' I shouted as I tipped the table up and flew across at him before he could at me. We wrestled to the floor and fortunately the altercation was swiftly broken up.

'He ain't Old Bill, you prat – he's been going to Chelsea for donkey's years,' intervened one bloke as we were pulled apart. Hasn't been for years, more like, but who was I to argue? Sensing public opinion moving in my direction, I strained at the leash towards my opponent.

'You ain't too welcome here, mate,' said someone else, at which his two companions offered to take him to their cabin. When they had gone, my first saviour told me he was from Hillingdon and he remembered me from the '70s. And he did, as he recalled where I was from and even reeled off some of the names of the crowd I used to go with.

When we settled back down for the last leg of the journey, Pete remonstrated with me.

'What did you do that for? What is such an insult about being called a copper? My old man was a copper.'

'I know, Pete. I've got no problem at all with the police. But say everyone in that bar had believed him because I didn't react in an aggressive way. I'd have been kicked to shit, and so would you three as well.'

I don't think Pete saw it that way. I think he thought I was being lairy. I thought I didn't have a choice.

We drove from the ferry port to Bruges, where we simply parked the car in the main square, grabbed our Adidas bags and went off in search of accommodation. We began to get worried when we found that all hotels and guest houses were fully booked or had been sufficiently frightened into not allowing

Englishmen in. Finally I approached a bed and breakfast on the square, produced a business card of a famous company I had worked for ten years earlier and we were in. There was some drawing of lots over who had to share the double bed with Woody, who, by his own admission, had a habit of wetting the bed after a night on the drink.

In the reception area we met up with three Glasgow Rangers fans who had also secured accommodation. They said that Chelsea was their second club and that they wouldn't have missed this match for the world. We invited them with us on our search for a ticket but they already had theirs. Whilst they were very pleasant, it was clear that they didn't fancy knocking around with us. They had their stay clearly planned out, having driven across Great Britain and Europe, and were not going to take any chances wandering around Bruges with ticketless Chelsea fans.

So on the afternoon of the game we set off in search of a ticket. The others had initially been dubious about travelling to the match without one but I had persuaded them. I was still stuck in the 'You can't ban a Chelsea fan' mentality. Years ago there was an initiative to prevent us travelling to away matches but we just turned up regardless and in even bigger numbers. The local constabularies were faced with the prospect of letting us into the ground or having five thousand Chelsea roaming the streets. They always chose the lesser of the two evils.

We found a bar on the edge of the square. The song that begins 'The famous Man United . . .' reverberated out through the door. Hearing this and other '60s/early '70s songs underlined the fact that the ghost of Chelsea past was very much present here in Belgium.

The bar was packed and very boisterous, so much so that two mounted Belgian police stood outside as if on sentry duty. One lowered his head until it was level with his horse's neck and said to us, 'Why don't you try one of the bars away from the square? They will welcome your custom.'

He spoke perfect English and we entered into a polite, relaxed conversation with him as we stroked his horse. But you know how it is when you can feel eyes boring into your back? I glanced over my shoulder and there, crushed up against the bay window of the packed pub, were my friends from Essex – and there were us three in apparent friendly (possibly conspiratorial) conversation with the local police! I have never felt more undercover in my life.

We did find another bar, where we fell into excited drinking with friends from home and others I hadn't seen for some years. Getting a ticket seemed less and less urgent as the alcohol buzz kicked in. But, conscious of the fact that when the bar emptied and we were the only ones left our low would be worse than the current high, Pommy and I set off to find tickets for the four of us.

Heading in the general direction of the ground, we were astounded by the numbers of Chelsea around. Every bar was heaving, with as many people hanging around outside as there were inside. I didn't pick up any vibes of trouble but I did wonder how, if things turned nasty, the police would cope.

Just by the stadium we were approached by two scruffy youths. They asked us in broken English if we were looking for tickets. I'd hoped they were touts but they directed us to a bar down the side of the ground. We found it and walked straight in. The bar was busy with young men looking very much like their English counterparts, talking in groups and drinking. The smell of marijuana was noticeable. Like in a scene from a Western film, the hubbub of conversation suddenly stopped and all eyes were on Pommy and me. No one rushed towards us proffering tickets, so we stepped up to the bar and ordered drinks. Eventually we were approached by a long-haired youth in a leather bomber jacket.

'Are you Chelsea's boys?'

I was worried that Pommy might fire back a cynical reply like 'Not all of them', so I quickly responded.

'No, we're just looking to buy a ticket. Two lads outside said we might get one in here.'

The Belgian laughed and said something to his companions and then the whole pub started to laugh too. It was obvious that we'd been set up. This was Bruges's firm in here and the two blokes outside had thought they'd send us to an uncertain fate for a laugh. We finished our drinks and left ticketless.

This stuff about 'Are you Chelsea's boys?' reminds me of a story my friend Simon told me. He is a lifelong Norwich City fan and during the '80s he got right into the England thing, travelling all over the world following the national side. He and his mates were in their early twenties and once found themselves on a plane sitting in a bank of seats opposite Icky and some pals. He said he was embarrassed because his mates had recognised Icky and were almost beside themselves to be in such close proximity to this fabled England supporter. When Icky leant forward and asked them who they followed, they were awestruck.

'Norwich,' answered Simon.

'Are you boys?' enquired Icky, looking along the tier of seats, and to Simon's eternal shame and embarrassment, his mate replied, 'Well, not really. I'm nineteen, but he's twenty-two and he's twenty-four.'

Even Icky was apparently momentarily speechless.

On the way back to our bar, it was clear that the atmosphere had changed. What I at first thought were tanks were encroaching towards where most Chelsea fans had congregated. I later learned these were army-type vehicles carrying water cannons. We saw police rounding up groups of fans and putting them on buses. At the time I thought they were just speeding up the process of getting them to the stadium, but I later found out that hundreds of these people had been taken to pens and held overnight. I never found out what had prompted this extreme reaction. I had seen no trouble anywhere.

Because we were heading in the opposite direction to the moving throng we were left alone and managed to get back into our bar. It was fairly full of locals and Chelsea fans without tickets who had heard about the police paranoia and didn't fancy it out on the streets. The manager of the bar was quite clued up and he laid down the law to each and every one of us.

'I will stay open as long as you like. But I am locking this door and no one gets in or out. So if you want to go somewhere else you go now. Also, as we have Bruges fans and Chelsea fans in here, I expect you to be friends whoever wins the match.' He pointed up at the television. 'We will watch the first half on Belgian TV and the second half on BBC with English commentary. Okay?'

And that is how it went. A great night.

There are two small postscripts to the story. Pommy and I were the two married ones among the group and at some point in the evening we did manage to nip out of the bar and phone our wives from one of the public telephones in the main square.

'Are you okay?' asked my wife in a very concerned voice.

'Of course I am. Why?'

'It says on the news that there are mass riots out there.'

'Not that I've seen.'

'Well, it's the headlines on the news. Hang on, I'll switch it over to Sky.'

She put the receiver near the TV and I could hear the reporter saying that there had been running battles in the main square between fans and police and that marauding Chelsea fans had smashed up the bars. Pommy and I surveyed the busy square. This was the main square. Barely a policeman in sight and certainly no running battles or smashed glass and trashed bars.

We rose early for breakfast despite drinking into the early hours. Woody wetting the bed had something to do with it. Our acquaintances from Glasgow were nowhere to be seen. I asked the manager what had happened to them. He told me that they had been on the phone from Dover, having been rounded up by the police and put on a ferry home. Apparently one was on his way back over to collect their car, which was still parked outside the bed and breakfast.

Around the square during the day we got to hear about the mass deportations and the holding of hundreds of fans in disused aircraft hangars. We were also told how television companies had been staging fights and rowdy behaviour for the cameras and how some crews had been attacked. Many fans blamed the television crews for whipping up the hysteria and prompting the extreme reactions from the authorities. Apparently this had changed the mood of the Chelsea followers and after a while it had become unsafe to be seen around town if you were connected with the satellite television companies in any way.

The only trouble I heard about between the fans was that apparently an old Chelsea face had burst into one of the bars where the Bruges mob were drinking. He had smiled at them, clicked his heels and thrown his arm in the air.

'Heil Hitler!'

They had lunged forward to get at him but he had simply taken a few backwards steps out of the door. They had followed him out, only to be pounced upon by the two lots of Chelsea who they should have guessed were waiting either side of the doorway.

* * *

Chelsea would need to win the home leg by at least 2–0 after the 1–0 defeat in Belgium. A good number of our boys were out for revenge after their experiences in Bruges, although it has to be said very little of it had been down to the opposing fans. Rumour had it that the Belgians would really be turning up.

'If that's the case,' I said to Roy, 'let's see if the Old Bill and customs turn them back at every point.'

'Yeah,' replied Roy, 'and I wonder if our police will turn water cannons on the ones who do get through and then cart them off to Heathrow and lock them in hangars all night.'

We laughed at the very thought. Our boys were sitting in a pub just off Carnaby Street, where they had arranged to meet because they had been assured that the Bruges lot would be drinking in a nearby pub off Regent Street. There were about fifty who were waiting for a few of the others who were meant to be in on this one.

'Fuck sitting around here – let's get off and find these tossers!' said one of our top faces. A couple of the lads said they'd have a scout around and be right back. Within minutes, they had returned.

'They're here!' they gasped, almost disbelievingly.

'How many?'

'Forty-handed at least.'

Everyone piled out and headed for the nearby pub, but the Belgians must have sussed the scouts because just as Chelsea arrived they saw the tail end of their boys scurrying away down a side street.

'This way,' hissed one of ours who knew London back-doubles like the back of his hand, being a motorbike messenger. After weaving their way through a few side streets in quick-march fashion, they turned a corner and ran straight into the startled Belgians. Our European friends just stood there wide-eyed with mouths agape. No water cannons or police dogs to protect them. They were well and truly in shit street – or was it Beak Street? To a man they fled, but only half of them managed to escape Chelsea dishing out their own version of European justice. Enthusiasm was such that Roy's brother was surrounded by snarling English, but they were soon put straight by Roy. The Europeans were prostrate and unconscious (or feigning unconsciousness) within seconds, so everyone set off to find the cowards who had allowed their fellow countrymen to get such a hiding. Swinging London must have been a lonely place for our frightened European cousins this cold winter's afternoon.

Lining the Fulham Road down at the ground were hundreds more Chelsea fans waiting for a Belgian contingent they knew in their hearts would not turn up. The police were the ones everyone had the grudge with, but the fans, or even the team and club officials, would have to do. And this was one occasion when the so-called hooligans and the so-called real fans were united in purpose. Roy nodded over at three Chelsea pensioners, smart but fragile in their red and black uniforms.

'They're here to get revenge for their seventy-two-year-old brother who got banged up in an industrial shed by the Bruges Old Bill,' he joked.

Chelsea won the game 2–0, putting us through to the semi-finals. Arsenal were also in the draw, so if we could avoid them in the semis, an all-English European Cup-Winners' Cup final was on the cards.

SPAIN IN THE NECK

We drew the Spanish club Real Zaragosa, with the first leg in Spain. Again my instincts (or was it my pocket?) told me to stay at home and again I was proven right. By all accounts, fans were subject to some of the most barbaric police assaults in memory. In Belgium the police had acted out of fear, inexperience and a post-Heysel paranoia. In Spain the police wanted to crack English skulls. Full stop. I heard countless stories of police attacking men, women and children with long truncheons just for sitting in the Chelsea-designated part of the ground. Their violence even surpassed the beatings they had visited on hundreds and hundreds of England supporters during the 1982 World Cup finals. Now, I don't mind a tear-up with anyone, but if someone is going to do me with a truncheon, I want to know who it is and I want to know I have some chance of retribution. I am not going to knowingly put myself forward as Spanish cosh fodder.

By all accounts, the fans behaved themselves impeccably on the day of the game and the police were laid back, jovial and friendly. But by nightfall the mood, again, had changed. Perhaps it was because the undercover officers of the Football

Intelligence Unit, conspicuous in their Hawaiian shirts and matching shorts (apparently they couldn't have been more obvious if they had ridden into town on donkeys, wearing sombreros and ponchos and sporting false moustaches), started pointing people out.

'That's Weller from Woking. One conviction, 1987, throwing celery on to the pitch at Birmingham.'

And the police, some wearing balaclavas, tore in. All very sinister.

John from Epsom told me that he was having a drink in a café bar near the ground with some mates when they heard a rumbling noise which was becoming louder and louder. On looking out they could see hundreds of Spanish fans, some banging on large drums which were hanging from their necks, marching down the middle of the road. Traffic was at a standstill as the procession moved onwards. The bar owner pleaded with John and his friends to come inside because if the Spanish fans realised the English were there they would wreck his life's toil. The Chelsea boys had little choice in the matter, though, because a wine bottle sailed through the air and smashed against the wall, missing John's nut by inches.

'You fucking wankers!' cried John as he stepped out into the road in front of the delegation. He cracked the nearest Spaniard to him on the jaw and stepped over him to take the next one out. All the boys from the bar came streaming out behind, pounding the home fans with plates of half-eaten paella and anything else they could lay their hands on. The distraught bar owner scurried out behind them with a long pole and pulled down the metal shutters at record speed, thereby depriving the Chelsea fans of further ammunition and a means of retreat. Twenty Chelsea on to hundreds of pissed-up Spaniards full of energy following their siesta didn't look too clever in the cold light of the day.

The Spanish fans, though, many who looked like '60s

revolutionaries with their long hair and goatee beards, had the numbers but not the bottle. They ran forward, lobbed beer and wine bottles and then retreated into their throng. The police arrived, screeching to a halt between the two factions, whilst the Spanish fans ran off in every direction. John and company thought the respite would be very welcome, but no such luck. These weren't peacekeepers – they were reinforcements!

John was battered to the floor by several batons and his hands were fastened behind his back with plastic straps. He was then lifted from the floor by the novel method of two truncheons beneath his chin whilst all the time taking body blows from other policemen. The back doors of the van opened and John knew that the hiding he was taking outside would look like sexual foreplay compared to what was going to happen behind closed doors. But, inexplicably, something changed their minds and they allowed him literally to roll off the bumper and land as a crumpled heap on the floor as they leapt back into their carrier and roared off. John was picked up and led to another bar, where the owner cut his straps with the knife he used for slicing lemons.

Inside the ground, the hostilities continued unabated. One Chelsea fan was grabbed and thrown to the floor before being publicly beaten and dragged out to the exits. Seconds before, he had been taking posed photos of his mates in the stand. Chelsea lost 3–0 but most people didn't give a fuck, self-preservation from the Old Bill being the priority.

Chelsea won the return leg 2–0 but it wasn't enough to take us to the final. The competition was eventually won by the Spaniards, after they defeated Arsenal with a last-minute goal. A hopeful whack by the ex-Spurs player Nayim from halfway caught the Gunners' keeper David Seaman off his line and sailed over him into the net. Shortly afterwards, Chelsea and Arsenal played at the Bridge and the Chelsea fans were quick to remind Seaman of his *faux pas*. Practically the whole ground stood and sang, 'Let's all do the Seaman, let's all do the Seaman, la la la la, la la la la,' as they held their arms aloft, flapping them helplessly at thin air.

Colin Ward, the literary Arsenal fan, said in his book *Steaming In* that the blackest day in Chelsea's terrace history was when they were spanked good and proper inside and outside White Hart Lane in the 1974–75 season. Well, this season, when Arsenal got run live on television by the Spanish beneath the Eiffel Tower and then had the piss taken out of Seaman up and down the country, must rank pretty low in their terrace existence thus far. Ward was right, though, about the Spurs débâcle in the mid-'70s. It still rankles now, especially with at least one of the old '70s leaders, who still reproaches himself over the last few games of cards in the pub that made his firm late and effectively condemned Chelsea's enthusiastic pups to a vicious spanking.

SLOVAKIA

A couple of seasons later we qualified for the Cup-Winners' Cup through the front door following our 2–0 defeat of Middlesbrough in the FA Cup final at Wembley. In the first round Chelsea were drawn against a Slovakian club and a substantial number of fans, mindful of their previous trip to that part of the world, decided to revisit. Most were glad they did, as the police and local people generally seemed glad to see them. Beer worked out at fifty pence per bottle and the dearest seat in the ground cost one pound.

ICE COLD IN TROMSO

As expected, Chelsea progressed to the next round, where they were drawn against Tromso, a Norwegian team who played their football somewhere up near the Arctic circle. Chelsea were unable to play their now distinctive passing game on the snow-covered pitch and the Norwegians got a well-deserved 3–2 victory. My mate Glen was one of the few hundred who braved the conditions and he said it was the coldest he had ever been, but I think it was the beer at seven pounds a pint that hurt more. The return leg on familiar terrain yielded a 7–1 trouncing of Tromso by the Blues, and a tie with Real Betis of Spain beckoned.

SPAIN AGAIN

Lots of fans booked holidays in the south of Spain to coincide with the game, driving up to Seville on the day of the match. This time the Spanish police fooled everyone by being unbelievably courteous and friendly. A British newspaper ran a piece about Chelsea fans attacking Betis fans before the game but the reality was that Chelsea were set upon by locals in the main square. A Spanish newspaper reported the correct version of events. Seville, the boys said, was a beautiful city that looked even better after Tore Andre Flo, Chelsea's very own Torchy the Battery Boy, scored twice to set us up nicely for the second leg, which we won comfortably.

ITALIAN JOB

Vicenza of Italy provided the opposition in the next round but the Italians only allocated Chelsea around a thousand tickets. Those who went said the police overreacted again, ferrying fans on to buses and then deliberately delivering them to the stadium after the match had begun. In the ground, those who sang or cheered got the now familiar rough end of a truncheon dug into their rib cage. But what else could be expected from the Italian police, who have a long history of abusing British football fans dating back well before the tragedy of Heysel.

Back at Stamford Bridge Chelsea had a one-goal deficit to recover, and prospects deteriorated further when the Italians went 1–0 up. Gus Poyet managed to pull one back and then we got another but Vicenza were still poised to go through on the away-goals rule. But then up popped Mark Hughes, in the twilight of his illustrious career, to score a fantastic goal to take us into the European Cup-Winners' Cup final for the first time since 1971. Stuttgart of Germany would be our opponents in the neutral city of Stockholm.

ZOLA POWER

I've decided to jet out to Stockholm as Glen has sorted me out an airline ticket and a match ticket. Well, he's wangled an airline ticket to Copenhagen and from there I have to pay for a flight between Copenhagen and Stockholm. Only seventy quid, he assures me. We're flying on the morning of the game and returning the morning after, so things promise to be a bit hectic, but I can't complain because it looks like Glen has sorted me an almost-free European excursion. He had the sense to fly out to Stockholm and buy tickets direct from the stadium, rather than paying the extortionate prices for the travel packages being offered by Chelsea and Hair Dryer Travel. The scousers and the Mancs were soon in on the act offering half-price deals, but I was happy to fly Glen Tours.

I drove to Glen's in the early hours, the intention being for me to leave my car at his house and then for us to drive to the airport in his. He'd leave his motor in the staff car park for the duration. As I pulled into his road, I could see him standing at the top of his drive ready and waiting. He had some idea about turning up earlier and getting on an SAS flight that would get us to Copenhagen two hours before the others.

'What others?'

'Oh, Jim Pike and a load of others are all on the British Midland flight.'

Everything went according to Glen's precision plan, and we even got upgraded into business class.

'Champagne?' enquired the pretty blonde hostess, leaning

over us, but, alas, there was no cleavage to be seen. Glen's nose twitched as the breakfast was deposited in front of him.

'You've always got to keep one step ahead of the rest,' he smirked as another sausage was popped into the cavernous black hole that was his mouth.

'Is that why you're thinking about dinner now?'

At Copenhagen, I joined the short queue at the SAS desk for my return ticket to Stockholm.

'How would you like to pay, sir?'

I pulled out the gold credit card that I had applied for weeks before. Every week junk mail poured through my door trying to get me to take a gold credit card. Me! I'd only just got my head around a bank account. I was quite disappointed when they accepted me – it made me realise that any prat could get one. I signed the slip and walked away.

'How much was that?'

I studied the slip and saw it said three thousand kroner. Glen took my arm and guided me away.

'What's that in real money?'

Glen tried to change the subject. I returned to the ticket counter and asked how much three thousand kroner was in real money.

'Two hundred and ninety-six pounds sterling,' the lady replied, smiling.

'Two hundred and ninety-six pounds? You're having a laugh!' I exclaimed. 'I'm going to fucking Stockholm, not Sydney.'

'It is first class, sir.'

'I didn't ask to go first fucking class!'

'That is the only ticket we do to Stockholm, I'm afraid. If you book twenty-eight days in advance you can have the economy ticket. If you stay seven days or longer you can have the cheap long-stay ticket, but if you go today and come back tomorrow the cheapest ticket is two hundred and ninety-six pounds.'

I turned around to glare at Glen. He shrugged his shoulders and lowered his head in an I-can't-help-it-and-please-don't-hit-me sort of way.

'Seventy quid you told me, Glen. This has cost me three hundred so far and I'm barely out of bed.'

'Sorry, Martin.'

'You're fucking sorry? I'm fucking sorry!'

'Calm down, Martin, people are staring.'

I looked to see who was staring so I had an excuse to jib someone.

'Let me buy you a drink.'

'Too right – you're buying all the drinks all today and all tomorrow!'

We got through customs and I sat down and waited for the drink Glen was hurriedly ordering at the bar. Looking up at the departure screen, I couldn't see anything listed for Stockholm.

'Don't worry,' said Glen. 'They'll be calling it soon.'

A couple of drinks later there was still no sign of a flight, so I suggested Glen enquired over at the SAS desk. Minutes later he was back.

'You won't believe this, Martin.'

'What?'

'Promise you won't hit me?'

'What?'

'The SAS engineers have gone on strike and they can't say when the next flight to Stockholm will be. I'm really sorry.'

Again I started effing and blinding whilst everyone else in the bar pretended not to hear. It didn't occur to me until afterwards that most of the airport probably thought we were a couple of old poofs having a series of lovers' tiffs.

'I don't believe this! I've paid two hundred and ninety-six quid to sit in a Copenhagen waiting-room when I could have paid four poxy quid more and got a hotel, flight and match ticket.'

Glen came back a few minutes later with what he thought was good news. The SAS rep had said we could wait in the business class lounge and help ourselves to food and drink. I kicked off with a small bottle of champagne, washed down with a cheeky red wine, and then moved on to the lobsters, crabs and prawns, washed down with a small bottle of Chablis. I then settled down to a production line of Heineken bottles. Jim Pike and his dad appeared in the lounge and Glen encouraged them to help themselves to food as if it was his own spread. We were just imparting our hard-luck story when a flight flashed up on the monitor. It was timed for another hour and Glen put down the lobster claw he was performing artificial respiration on and led us through to another lounge. More drink. I started with a small bottle of champagne and washed it down with a small bottle of Mateus.

As we boarded I barged in front of the others and took a seat in business class whilst they were dumped in the more familiar scumbag class. The hostess offered me a neatly pressed *Financial Times* to read, apologising for not having the *Sun* that I had asked for. The flight was a short one and we were landing at Stockholm Airport before I'd got beyond page two of the pink paper.

At customs everyone was allowed through except me. Police with guns led me away to a little cubicle and had a cursory rummage through my holdall.

'Are you here for the football?' asked the best-looking one who, I began to realise through my alcoholic haze, was a woman. They handed me a strange little leaflet that said something like 'Stockholm police welcome Chelsea fans but please don't piss in the street'.

Glen and the others assumed I was on some sort of Interpol list of wanted criminals and quizzed me up as to what had happened in the cubicle.

'Don't worry,' I reassured them out the corner of my

mouth. 'I didn't give anything away. Just told them my name, rank and number over and over again.'

They looked at me like I was off my head – which, by now, I was.

Jumping on the bus to the city centre, I was surprised at what a beautiful sunny day it was and puzzled for some time over why every car on the road had its fog lights on. I was filled with a sense of well-being and I just knew that tonight Chelsea would be parading the European Cup-Winners' Cup in front of their fans.

The arrangement had been to meet my cousin Mark and some of the other lads in an Irish bar called the Dubliners. I was concerned that as we were three hours behind schedule they might have fucked off by now. But as we walked in we could just have been beamed into any pub within a mile of Stamford Bridge on a match day. Mark was there, already the worse for wear, as were Martin Knight, Chris Mallows and John King. Jerry Kilburn and half a dozen paddies trooped in soon after and started ordering pints of Guinness by the dozen. They kept ordering and asked the barman to put the pints in the bin. This enabled all of us to confuse the bar staff and continue drinking the black staff long after the 'bin' had run dry.

I knew things were falling apart when Mark jumped on the table and started playing the spoons. 'My old man said be a Chelsea fan' was what he was supposed to be rendering, and although it was just a drunken clattering of cutlery, the whole pub caught on and Mark had his fifteen minutes of fame. He was most put out when I dragged him by the scruff of the neck to the taxi rank after deciding it was time to get off to the ground. Outside he pounced on three pretty blondes who had probably just finished at the office and press-ganged them into having their photos taken with us. They were good sports and agreed.

On the way to the stadium we passed another bar equally

full of Chelsea fans. We told the driver to drop us off and we'd walk the rest of the way. Paul Elliott, the ex-Chelsea player, was in the bar with a Radio 5 Live commentary team. Behaviour outside was boisterous but the police looked on with quiet amusement. I think the fact that many of their number were women, and pretty ones at that, prevented any animosity from building up. The guns strapped to their waists might also have contributed. On the last short walk to the stadium we ran into Peter Osgood and Ronnie Harris, running the gauntlet of drunken but nevertheless amiable Chelsea fans. It struck me as very fitting that they should be here.

A German mob of around forty were spotted scurrying down a subway but no one seemed very interested. This was a Chelsea day, not a rucking day. Mind you, the Germans thought differently. As they emerged from the subway, they broke into a strange chant of 'Deutschland, Deutschland Hooligan'. There was no specific Chelsea firm waiting to engage them but clumps of interested fans simply broke off from whomever they were with and ran into the Krauts from all angles. The Stuttgart fans had been testing the water and got their result quicker than they had figured.

Although in the confusion outside the ground we had all got split up, I soon found Glen in the seats. We were positioned just below the Stuttgart fans, who were obviously in a tiny minority. Chelsea fans packed every inch of the stadium save this little island reserved for the Germans. There must have been twenty thousand Chelsea here and perhaps five thousand more still in the town, either ticketless or preferring to stay in the bars and hotels. I wondered who was here. How many of the people who had attended the Spurs game at Stamford Bridge in 1968 were at this game? How many who had gone to the 1970 cup final were here? Who had died along the way? How many had struggled against comfortable middle age and its trappings to see

Chelsea, their old club – whose result they look out for on a Saturday afternoon but little else these days – come full circle and take the European Cup-Winners' Cup for the second time? Was Greenaway here? I hadn't heard a Zigger Zagger all day and really we should have. This should be his night as well. He was a supporter extraordinaire, as much a part of the Chelsea culture as Ossie, and he was definitely here. And all the others of the old guard, some now old enough to be fighting for the Home Guard – had they made the trip? Some, I know, are embarrassed, even ashamed, about their Chelsea past, but they knew this would be the last time any of them could show out and I thought they would. One last time. Someone said Eccles was here with an entourage. I doubted it but wished it was true. I wanted to see anyone and everyone who had clumped and been clumped for Chelsea. Tonight would give us some validity, I felt, some reason for thirty years of traipsing around the country following a thankless team and a club that didn't want us. We owed each other a lot, and tonight should be the seal on it all.

It was a tedious game until Zola came on as substitute and scored. It was almost in the script. The game ended and the ground erupted. Despite a high-wire fence surrounding the pitch, Chelsea fans streamed on and the players seemed genuinely pleased to share their celebrations with them. I spotted one of Babsy's old boys tearing over to Dennis Wise, niftily dodging the stewards, with half of his trousers left flapping on the barbed-wire fence. For a good twenty minutes the fans cheered, clapped and sang before Dennis the Menace finally trotted up to accept the trophy. The symmetry of it all.

Outside the ground, the fickleness of the Chelsea fans was again apparent. The atmosphere was flat. No singing. No chanting. No excited chatter. By their manner, anyone would have thought they were returning from a 0–0 draw with Wimbledon at Plough Lane. We filed on to an underground train, and still the atmosphere was subdued. The platform at each station we stopped at was lined with Stockholm police. They had their riot helmets hanging from their belts, along with a gun, a truncheon, handcuffs and a canister containing what I suspected was CS gas. They had more paraphernalia wrapped around them than Batman could boast on his utility belt. But still they didn't adopt threatening poses. Some rode on the train with us and their whole body language signified, 'We are the same as you. You happen to be a mechanic. I happen to be a policeman.' In England, as most of us know (football hooligan or no football hooligan), the whole demeanour is, 'I am a policeman and you are the people I am policing. I am superior to you. I am right; you are wrong.' There is much talk these days of the police in Britain being institutionally racist. That misses the point. The police are institutionally arrogant. They are no more corrupt or racist than the rest of us but arrogance underpins their whole ethos. I think their service has traditionally attracted people who are not very intelligent and who hold no burning ambitions in life. Through joining the police force they can exercise control over others and attain a degree of peer-group respect they would not normally be able to achieve. Long service ensures that some of these people rise to the top, and therefore you have inadequate people dealing with situations and policies that would test the most skilled operators in public life.

Back in the town centre, it soon became apparent that most bars had shut up, a strange decision considering there were twenty-five thousand Chelsea fans wandering around aimlessly. Eventually we found an Italian restaurant which was open, on account of Zola scoring, perhaps. Sitting at a table outside was a face from the past. He stretched out his arm, stood up and walked towards me.

'How ya doing?'

'I'm great, Babsy. You're looking well.'

Besides the greying of his hair, he looked no different from the bloke we had followed, and who had become our friend, twenty-five years before. We had a drink together and chatted about the old days. Times had changed, he said. He invited me back to the hotel around the corner where he was staying with a group of his old lot, but I declined as I fancied some nosebag. I watched them meander off to the hotel, ribbing and taking the piss out of one another like middle-aged men from the local working-man's club out on a beano to Margate. Which is, of course, what they were.

I asked one of the others if another old mucker of ours was out here.

'Na, he's been ill. Had cancer of the bollocks.'

From fighting Arsenal to testicular cancer in fifteen short years. It made me quite depressed.

We found a kebab shop and sat there eating, chatting and drinking till the early hours. Eventually scoutmaster Glen said it was time to hit the airport. The cabbie was a Lebanese man studying to be an English teacher in Stockholm and, surprise, surprise, he supported Manchester United.

The terminus was awash with Chelsea fans. The first two of the charter flights had been cancelled and the airport was almost out of control. Confused police tried to keep order, breaking up the bigger groups and attempting to keep people moving. But there was nowhere to move to. At one point Ronnie Harris came walking across the terminus. He was loudly applauded and the roar of 'There's only one Chopper Harris' drowned out the public-address system. He looked down at the floor in embarrassed silence. I could see he was touched. Did you think we'd forget you, Ron?

Eventually we found another departure lounge, made makeshift beds from the cushions of a closed restaurant and tried to nick a couple of hours' shuteye.

'Martin King, I don't believe it!'

I looked up and beaming down at me was Gary. I had neither seen nor heard of him for twenty years. He was always a barrel of laughs. Straight away I remembered a game at Manchester City when he was wearing a Prince Charles mask as we were being escorted to the ground.

'Get that mask off!' ordered a policeman who rode up alongside him.

'Why? You're wearing one.'

It was a reply that had earned Gary a crack across the forehead with a truncheon.

'Fuck me, Gary! How are you?'

The F-word seemed to make him wince. A young lady stood behind him, smiling sweetly.

'I suppose you're here for the football?'

'Ain't you?'

'No, we've been to a seminar. We're on our way back to California.'

'California? What you doing in fucking California?'

'Martin, ease up on the old swearing,' he said, gently nodding towards his friend, who continued to study me with a fixed smile. 'I live in California. I'm with the Scientologists now.'

'You what?'

'The Church of Scientology, Martin. Have you not heard of it?'

I had. I was dumbstruck. Gary had always been a bit of a nutter, but he'd been on some journey. From Crawley to California. From National Front to Church of Scientology. He pressed a leaflet into my hand bearing a picture of John Travolta and wrote down his address and phone number.

'If you are ever passing through, drop in and see us.'

'Yeah, I pass through California a lot. Who's us anyway? D'you live on a fucking commune or something?'

He just smiled, then pulled me towards him and hugged me.

'You never change, Kingy, do you?'

Glen had by now woken from his slumber, and I could see that the sight of this well-dressed, well-spoken and well-manicured man embracing me confused him. Gary and his friend departed, leaving me to fall back to sleep and ponder this strange interlude.

The next thing I remember is waking to feel a Rottweiler dog sniffing my genital area. The policeman at the other end of the lead jerked him away. The dog moved over to explore the crack of Glen's arse, which was protruding from the top of his jeans. I noticed a smile spread across Glen's face.

At six o'clock Glen's alarm went off on his prized diver's watch. We went to the desk and handed our tickets over. I was told I would probably get on this flight if any of the business class customers did not show but the others were told to try their luck with the massive throng of Chelsea in the departure area. I was called and the cold hams and cheeses and the reclining seat with plenty of leg room were most welcome. I did run into Glen at Copenhagen Airport, and from there we finally got our flight to Heathrow. By the time we got into Glen's car we were both physically and mentally drained. As we turned into his road, a huge sigh from him jolted me out of my half-awake, half-asleep state. His house was bedecked with Chelsea flags and scarves, which were hanging from the windows and the trees in the garden. His mum hurried out into the drive to greet us.

'Welcome home, boys! Do you like the bunting?'

'Yes, Mum. Thanks, Mum,' he said.

Red with embarrassment, he dashed for the door. This cheered me up no end and made everything worth while. I chuckled to myself all the way home thinking about the real-life Frankie Abbott – mummy's little soldier.

My abiding memory of the day, though, is the scene at the end of the match. Twenty thousand Chelsea fans rocked from side to side, arms outstretched, mimicking aeroplanes and humming the theme from *The Dambusters*. It was our greatest moment for a quarter of a century but uppermost in the Chelsea mind was to wind up the few Germans present in the stadium.

But we'd won the Cup-Winners' Cup and for me this was the end of a long journey. This was more or less where I had come in thirty years back. It was time to get on with the rest of my life.

The Millennium Thug

'Some clubs are considering opening singing and non-singing areas within their stadiums.'

Daily Mail, 1996

Early 1999. Manchester United and Liverpool fans had their planned battle rumbled by a national newspaper hours before the meet was due to take place. A van parked close to the ground was found to contain an array of weapons including petrol bombs, Stanley knives, baseball bats and iron bars.

Weeks later, across the other side of Manchester, Millwall fans turned up at Maine Road in the biggest numbers seen in years. Never had so many travelled out of Bermondsey together since the halcyon days of hop picking. Stockport was the venue for the pre-arranged morning meet and this was advertised widely on the Internet. Man U fans travelled to Stockport on their way to Nottingham and Millwall on their way to Manchester City. Millwall fans allegedly destroyed a whole street of mainly Indian restaurants before engaging the locals in fights before, during and after the game. One police officer commented that he had not seen so much trouble at a football match in his twenty-five years of service. His colleague, a senior officer responsible for anti-hooligan strategies within ACPO (Association of Chief Police Officers), said, 'Hooliganism is alive and well. Our problem is to keep a lid on it. The people involved in these groups are not stupid. They are extremely cunning.'

Well, it took thirty years, but that is the first time I have seen a policeman acknowledge in print that football thugs are not the brainless idiots they have traditionally been depicted as.

A few weeks later, West Bromwich Albion and Bristol City fans clashed in traditional 1970s style inside the ground. The fighting across the seats was broadcast by Sky Sports as they waited several minutes to film the game. The footage clearly showed the stewards frightened and completely helpless as the two factions tore into one another. It was suggested that the trouble had raged so freely because the home team had elected not to use police and to employ stewards instead. According to Albion secretary Dr John Evans, 'It was decided not to police the game as there didn't seem to be any potential difficulties.' I have thought for a long time that total stewarding of matches is a disaster waiting to happen.

These last two incidents received little or no media exposure. Had they happened in the '70s or '80s there would have been inquests, hand-wringing and calls to bring back hanging. There is, without doubt, some form of news blackout on hooligan activities and this, along with the conflicting messages from the authorities, makes a rational diagnosis of the state of play very difficult.

One day we hear that football violence is under control but it is a hell of a job to keep a lid on it. Then we hear that the problem is practically eradicated. And finally we hear it is back with a vengeance. The official view is usually that there are a few old dinosaurs around but that football stadiums are now completely safe places to be. Tell that to the crowds at Maine Road or the Hawthorns during the 1998–99 season.

Up until recently I subscribed to the theory that football

hooliganism was in its death throes but now I'm not so sure. I thought that if the press carried on ignoring it, the lack of new boys coming through would eventually ensure its extinction. But the above incidents seem to indicate that this may not be the case.

I believe that the current scenario runs something like this:

- Clashes between rival fans at Premiership grounds have been eliminated. This is down to all-seater stadiums, pricing and the emergence of 'new fans' as the predominant culture, top-flight football having been sold into new markets. These economic factors have achieved what years of undercover police work could not.

- Premiership clubs still have firms, albeit all of them are far smaller than ten, twenty or thirty years ago. They remain active but pick their clashes carefully and with the prior agreement of rival firms. Almost without exception, these confrontations take place away from the stadiums.

- Nationwide League grounds still witness outbreaks of fighting, although most of this goes unreported in the press at national level. Some of the firms are actually growing and attracting new blood. This is underlined by the emergence of the likes of Stoke City, Barnsley and Stockport as serious mobs in recent years.

- Lower-league and non-league football are attracting committed hooligans who find it is too 'hot' or there is not enough action with their original high-profile firm.

At this point in time I would argue that football hooliganism is no longer the national pastime for young people it once undoubtedly was. But it is still there in pockets and with a much higher level of commitment shown by those who indulge. Once it was a majority fashion; now it is a minority passion.

My point about the big old mobs meeting miles away from the grounds, sometimes hours before or after games, raises a question over whether 'football hooliganism' is the right term for it these days. To classify these as football problems is now a bit complacent, or disingenuous, in my view. Think about it: the violence involves gangs of men in their twenties, thirties and forties bashing shit out of each other with not a football in sight. Say five men drive out from London to Sussex on a fishing trip. On the way home they stop in a village pub and have a few drinks. They get into an argument with some locals and a fight breaks out. One man in each group is wearing a football shirt. Is this soccer-related violence? Add it to the list of social problems we currently face, by all means, but to allow it to be swept under football's carpet is wrong.

I've said it before, but those fishermen would end up with a fifty-pound fine at the local magistrates' court – if anyone bothered charging them. Had they done the same thing in a football stadium, they would probably have been jailed. Form or no form. Shout, swear or, God forbid, do the wankers sign in a Premiership ground these days and you'll find yourself looking at a fine with three noughts on the end.

Like the motorist, the football fan is seen as an easy target for the police. In both cases they can produce a steady stream of convictions, yielding a healthy income for the public coffers. How many times have you seen them jumping out of the shadows with their silly little guns and pulling some bugger over for speeding? When he or she has stopped they swarm over the car like ants. What is all this about? The cost of the operation is high, so the result (i.e. the income) has to be equally high. Why we as a society tolerate this is beyond me. We pay from our taxes for a police force that chooses to spend our money on policing non-crime and taxing us again, in the form of fines, for their fun and games.

I labour the analogy about the motorist simply because more people may be able to relate to it. But the fact is, in my opinion, that the same dynamics apply to football violence and the police. The hooligan is a soft target all right. Hooligans can be presented to the public as dangerous criminals and therefore it can appear to the public at large that the police are doing sterling and courageous work crossing swords with them. The reality is very different, as I hope our books have illustrated.

Anyone who has attended football regularly over the last thirty years will know it is not true. There really has never been a malevolent network of right-wing maniacs bent on causing anarchy. There have been large groups of young men, full of testosterone and drink, trying to outwit the police in order to confront each other. These, though, are simple crowd problems. As unpleasant and dangerous as they may be, they are controllable by good old-fashioned policing. So the police have homed in on soccer miscreants, as they have motoring miscreants, as a source of good public relations and a source of good money, the penalties being far beyond the gravity of the crime. 'Processing' is what they call it, I'm told. And just in case someone asks questions somewhere, it has to be presented and reaffirmed as this dark force that pervades society. Thank God the good old police are fighting it tooth and nail. And three cheers for the Football Intelligence Unit. Those busy bees beavering away in the offices of the National Criminal Intelligence Service. Sifting all that intelligence, pre-empting revolutions, analysing trends. Do me a favour – the only busy department at the FIU is the press office!

The following story sums them up for me. When trouble broke out at the World Cup in 1998 they were quoted as saying something like, 'This has surprised us . . . there are many people here who are not known to us . . . young people as well.' Now if someone from the FIU really said this, they were either trying to make excuses for the fact that they don't have any intelligence to speak of, or they really meant it. If they really meant it and were genuinely surprised, well, what can you say? If they actually believe that football violence is tightly harmonised and carried out by the same group of people then they have learnt absolutely nothing in thirty years. It was blindingly obvious from the television pictures that the blokes on display in France were, on the whole, ordinary guys from ordinary towns, on the piss and fired up by a hungry media into swearing, throwing bottles and acting in a disorderly fashion. And – dear, dear – these lads were not on the FIU's computer! Where does it all end?

An item in my local paper recently caught my eye. A youth had been taken to court for cycling on a footpath. A policeman turned up in court and gave evidence against the boy. The judge duly fined the lad twenty pounds. The boy, showing a sense of humour, asked if he could have time to pay, explaining that he had just spent all his money on a two-month holiday in Australia. The judge appreciated his cheek and allowed him seven days. Just imagine this boy was on the FIU computer. Would some undercover officers have been dispatched to Australia to monitor his activities? To ensure he didn't ride down any Sydney footpaths?

On a less flippant note, will a Cricket, Boxing or Horse-racing Intelligence Unit be set up now that disorder appears to be on the increase in these sports? What about a Nuts Secreted in Food Intelligence Unit, or a Pay Your Paper Bill on Time Unit, or a Food Past Its Sell-By Date Task Force?

And what about the geezer who sits in his office with a notice on his door saying 'Stupid names for ongoing operations'?

'Hello, guv. I'm from Essex Constabulary. We've had a teenager go missing from Frinton. I'm starting to drip-feed the media so I need a name for the investigation. I was thinking of "Operation Essex Girl". What do you think?'

The Namemaster General looks up from the porn magazine he has tucked inside a copy of the *Police Review*. 'No, we've used that. What about "Operation Budgie's Arse"? That'll suggest there could be more to it than just a missing-persons investigation.'

'That's great, guv. That'll keep the slags guessing.'

So it'll carry on. In the same way that young men fighting in pubs will carry on, or people killing themselves (and others), or people driving cars too fast or too drunkenly. It'll carry on because of vested interests and it'll carry on because violence is an obsession of the Western world. I was raised on a diet of violence. Papers screaming about Teddy boys razoring cinema seats, then Mods smashing Rockers over the heads with deckchairs, then skinheads running amok at football. Images from the Vietnam war formed the backdrop to my childhood. TV programmes like *The Sweeney* and *Minder* provided my adolescent entertainment. And I'm meant to go to a football ground and experience the electricity of rivalry, the thrill of the chase and the power of the crowd and not get hooked?

In Italy the clubs have taken it upon themselves to talk to the fans to see if they can come up with solutions to football violence. Fair play to them. Can you imagine clubs in this country talking to their fans? They'd rather tread in shit. I know of one Premier League club chairman who called the fans 'fucking whingers' in private, complaining to his staff about how he had improved the amenities and ambience at great cost and now all they did was moan.

They moan because their sport has been stolen from them. Going to football has always been a working-class passion. And you don't have to be poor to be working class. Some of the working class can't get work; some have enough money they don't need to work. Working class is a state of mind formed by heritage. But football belongs to us, not to big business, and one day it'll be reclaimed – or tossed back to us when it has been bled dry.

Football is what we like to do on a Saturday and it's what our older brothers, fathers and grandfathers liked to do too. Most of us enjoyed the soccer as well.